KB047179

중학 영어의 결정적 단어들

콜로케이션

저자 김경하

서강대학교 영문과를 졸업하고 American University에서 TESOL 석사학위를 취득 후, Stoddert Elementary School Volunteer 교사, Spring Hill Elementary School Volunteer 교사, YBM-Sisa Education 강사를 거쳐 현재 부모 및 교사 교육 강연과 영어교재 개발 중이다. 웅진씽크빅 유아 영어교재인 <Cookie Coo> 시리즈와 Bricks 영어교재인 <Spotlight on Literacy>를 기획자문 및 집필하기도 했다.

대표 저서
<Sight Words 1, 2>, <Picture Descriptions>, <Book Reports>, <Journal Writing>,
<초등 영어를 결정하는 영단어>, <초등 영어를 결정하는 영어표현>, <초등 영어를 결정하는 사이트워드>,
<초등 5, 6학년 영어에서 놓치면 안 되는 것들>, <중학 영어의 결정적 단어들_반의어> 등

**중학 영어의
결정적 단어들** 콜로케이션

저자 김경하

초판 1쇄 인쇄 2023년 12월 19일
초판 1쇄 발행 2023년 12월 28일

발행인 박효상 편집장 김현 기획・편집 장경희, 김효정 디자인 임정현
교정・교열 진행 홍윤영 표지・내지 디자인 Moon-C design 마케팅 이태호, 이전희 관리 김태옥
종이 월드페이퍼 인쇄・제본 예림인쇄・바인딩 녹음 YR미디어

출판등록 제10-1835호 발행처 사람in
주소 04034 서울시 마포구 양화로 11길 14-10 (서교동) 3F
전화 02) 338-3555(代) 팩스 02) 338-3545
E-mail saramin@netsgo.com
Website www.saramin.com

책값은 뒤표지에 있습니다. 파본은 바꾸어 드립니다.

ⓒ 김경하 2023

ISBN
979-11-7101-016-5 64740
979-11-7101-014-1 (set)

우아한 지적만보, 기민한 실사구시 **사람in**

중학 영어의 결정적 단어들

콜로케이션

김경하 지음

사람in
saram
in.com

외국어 학습의 가장 중요한 두 축은 정확성(accuracy)과 유창성(fluency)입니다. 그중 유창성이란 막힘없이 술술 하고 싶은 말을 해내는 것을 말합니다. 외국어 학습에서 이 유창성을 키우기 힘든 이유는 모국어와는 달리 머릿속에서 따로 한 번 더 바꿔 생각한 다음 말하는 과정이 필요하기 때문입니다. '나는 샤워를 했다'를 영어로 표현하려면 머릿속에서 다음의 과정을 거칩니다. 주어 다음에 어떤 동사를 써야 하지? shower 앞에는 a를 써야 하나? 참, 과거이니까 동사 과거형을 써야겠구나…. 짧은 순간에 머릿속에 여러 번의 생각이 지나가야 I took a shower.가 만들어집니다. 그래서 자연스럽게 문장을 만들기 힘들고, 줄줄이 이어 말하기는 더 힘들어지죠.

따라서 자주 쓰는 표현을 덩어리(chunk)로 외우는 것은 유창성을 키우는 가장 효과적인 방법입니다. 이것이 습관이 되면, 단어를 한 개씩 외워 따로따로 맞추어 문장을 만드는 것과는 비교가 되지 않을 만큼 빠르고 정확하게 영어를 쓸 수 있게 됩니다. 그래서『중학 영어의 결정적 단어들』2탄은 최고 빈출 동사 12개와 빈출 동사 60개, 형용사 36개, 부사 20개와 연결하여 익힐 수 있는 덩어리 표현, 즉 콜로케이션(collocation)을 다룹니다. 앞서 예로 들었던 '나는 샤워를 했다'는 '샤워하다'를 take a shower로 덩어리째 외워 두었다면 생각하는 시간을 줄여 바로 문장을 말할 수 있죠. 이 책에서는 빈출 표현, 구동사, 숙어, 관용구 등 자주 함께 사용되는 짝꿍 단어들을 넓은 범위에서 다양하게 만나게 될 것입니다.

언어를 모국어나 제2 언어로 접한다면 충분히 듣고 말할 기회를 통해서 자연스럽게 이 덩어리 표현을 익히게 될 것입니다. 하지만 우리 아이들이 영어를 배우는 환경, 즉 영어를 외국어로 배우는 EFL(English as a Foreign Language) 환경에서는 이 또한 잘 조절된 학습활동을 통해 습득해야 합니다. 그래서 이 책은 다음과 같이 구성되어 있습니다.

① 초등 고학년에서 중등으로 넘어가는 단계 또는 중등 1, 2학년 단계의 학교 수행평가나 지필 시험, 학원의 작문, 말하기 과제에 필요한 빈출 단어들과 그에 연관된 빈출 표현들을 선정하여 정리하였습니다. 목표 단어와 표현을 부각하기 위해 부정관사는 Expressions 파트에서는 뺐고, 대신 예문과 리뷰 문제들을 통해 충분히 접할 수 있습니다.

② 모든 단어와 표현들은 학습자가 따로 외워 문제를 푸는 것이 아닌, 문장 속에서 해당 표현을 따라 써 보며 자연스럽게 익힐 수 있도록 했습니다. 단어나 표현만을 따로 달달 외우면 당장은 더 많이 외울 수 있다고 착각할 수 있지만 실제로 꺼내어 쓸 수 없다면 시간 낭비에 불과할 테니까요. 그뿐만 아니라 예문으로 제시되는 문장들은 그 자체로 아이들이 말하기나 작문에 사용할 수 있어서 자연스럽게 몰입하고 학습의 동기도 높일 수 있습니다.

③ 단어→표현→문장 단계로 익힌 단어와 표현, 문장들은 다양한 액티비티를 통해 자연스럽게 암기가 되도록 했습니다. 아이들이 혼동하거나 실수하기 쉬운 부분을 활용한 액티비티부터 스스로 문장을 만들어 보는 것까지 단계적인 문제 풀이 활동을 제시했습니다. 다양한 문제 풀이 과정을 통해 단어를 인식하고 효과적으로 외우는 것은 물론, 이후 문법 시험 대비를 위한 꼼꼼한 시선도 훈련할 수 있도록 했습니다.

콜로케이션 학습은 apple은 '사과'하는 식으로 단어를 외워 온 친구들에게는 낯설고 더딘 과정이 될 것입니다. 하지만 최고 빈출 단어들을 짝꿍 단어들과 함께 외워 두면 말하기, 쓰기는 물론 독해할 때도 속도가 쑥쑥 느는 것을 경험하게 될 것입니다.

김경하

구성 및 특징

자주 쓰는 표현을 덩어리(chunk)로 외워 유창성을 키우는 재미있는 단어 책!

Expressions

핵심 단어가 들어가는 표현들을 그림과 함께 알아본다.
원어민 발음을 듣고 따라 읽으며 체화한다.

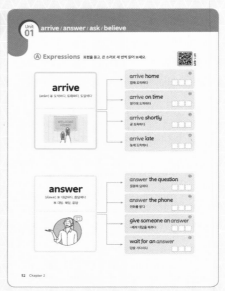

Check the Expressions

표현이 문장 속에서 어떻게 활용되는지
원어민의 목소리를 들으며 귀와 눈으로 익힌다. 직접 써 보며
손의 감각으로도 기억한다. 틀리게 쓰거나 주의해야 할 경우도 짚어 준다.

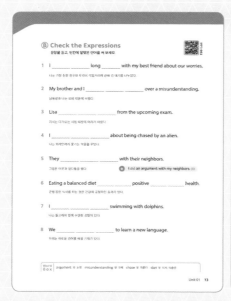

Review the Expressions

다양한 문제를 통해 앞에서 배운
표현들을 잘 이해하고 있는지 확인한다.

Expression Check List

각 Chapter에서 배운 표현들을 얼마나
암기하고 있는지 체크해 본다.

정답

각 Unit의 Check the Expressions와
Review the Expressions 문제의 답을
확인한다.

목 차

머리말

구성 및 특징

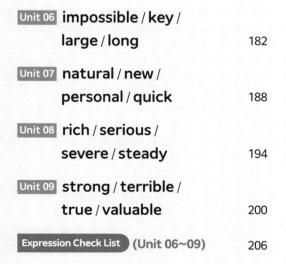

Chapter 1

최다빈출동사와
영어표현

have [hæv] 동 가지다, 있다, 소유하다, 먹다, (경험을) 하다, 받다
had - had

Ⓐ Expressions 표현을 듣고, 큰 소리로 세 번 읽어 보세요.

MP3-001

❶ ☑ ☐ ☐

have a chat
대화를[잡담을] 하다

❷ ☐ ☐ ☐

have a fight
싸우다

❸ ☐ ☐ ☐

have a headache
두통이 있다

❹ ☐ ☐ ☐

have a nightmare
악몽을 꾸다

❺ ☐ ☐ ☐

have an argument
말다툼하다

❻ ☐ ☐ ☐

have an effect (on)
(~에) 영향을 끼치다,
효과를 나타내다

❼ ☐ ☐ ☐

have an experience
경험하다

❽ ☐ ☐ ☐

have an opportunity
기회를 갖다

Ⓑ Check the Expressions

문장을 듣고, 빈칸에 알맞은 단어를 써 보세요.

1 I _____ _____ long _____ with my best friend about our worries.

나는 가장 친한 친구와 우리의 걱정거리에 관해 긴 얘기를 나누었다.

2 My brother and I _____ _____ _____ over a misunderstanding.

남동생과 나는 오해 때문에 싸웠다.

3 Lisa _____ _____ _____ from the upcoming exam.

리사는 다가오는 시험 때문에 머리가 아프다.

4 I _____ _____ _____ about being chased by an alien.

나는 외계인에게 쫓기는 악몽을 꾸었다.

5 They _____ _____ _____ with their neighbors.

그들은 이웃과 말다툼을 했다.

★ I ~~did~~ an argument with my neighbors. (X)

6 Eating a balanced diet _____ _____ positive _____ _____ health.

균형 잡힌 식사를 하는 것은 건강에 긍정적인 효과가 있다.

7 I _____ _____ _____ swimming with dolphins.

나는 돌고래들과 함께 수영한 경험이 있다.

8 We _____ _____ _____ to learn a new language.

우리는 새로운 언어를 배울 기회가 있다.

Word Box | argument 명 논쟁 misunderstanding 명 오해 chase 동 뒤쫓다 diet 명 식사, 식습관

take [teik] 통 가지다, 받다, 데려가다, 수강하다, 타다
took - taken

Ⓐ Expressions 표현을 듣고, 큰 소리로 세 번 읽어 보세요.

❶ ☐☐☐

take a class
수업을 듣다

❷ ☐☐☐

take an exam
시험을 치다

❸ ☐☐☐

take advantage of
~을 이용하다

❹ ☐☐☐

take a taxi 택시를 타다

❺ ☐☐☐

take notes
필기를 하다

❻ ☐☐☐

take a risk
위험을 감수하다

❼ ☐☐☐

take part (in)
(~에) 참여하다

❽ ☐☐☐

take place 열리다, 개최되다

Ⓑ Check the Expressions

문장을 듣고, 빈칸에 알맞은 단어를 써 보세요.

 MP3-004

1 I decided to _____ _____ _____ on coding.

나는 코딩 수업을 듣기로 결심했다.

2 Are you ready to _____ _____ _____?

너는 시험 볼 준비가 됐니?

3 We can _____ _____ _____ social networking service (SNS).

우리는 사회관계망서비스(SNS)를 이용할 수 있다.

4 He had to _____ _____ _____ to get there on time.

그는 그곳에 제시간에 도착하기 위해 택시를 타야 했다.

5 Many college students are _____ _____ on laptops.

많은 대학생들이 노트북에 필기를 하고 있다. ⭐ **People** took note of **his talents.** 알아챘다

6 _____ _____ _____ can lead you to new opportunities.

위험을 감수하는 것은 너를 새로운 기회로 이끌 수 있다.

7 Volunteers _____ _____ _____ the community cleanup event.

자원봉사자들은 마을 대청소 행사에 참여했다.

8 Our school festival will _____ _____ in May.

우리 학교 축제는 5월에 열릴 것이다.

Word Box | opportunity 몡 기회   volunteer 몡 자원봉사자   community 몡 지역 사회, 공동체   cleanup 몡 대청소

A 다음 문장의 빈칸에 공통으로 들어가는 단어를 써 보세요.

1 I _____ a chat with my friends. (과거형)

   I _____ an experience visiting Paris. (과거형)

2 I'm not ready to _____ an exam.

   The music festival will _____ place in July.

B <보기>에 주어진 단어를 이용하여 다음의 표현을 완성하세요.

보기
take effect risk have of
argument on advantage

1 논쟁하다   _____ an _____

2 ~에 영향을 미치다 _____ an _____ _____

3 ~을 이용하다   _____ _____ _____

4 위험을 감수하다   _____ a _____

C 다음 중 옳은 표현이 사용된 문장에는 O, 그렇지 않은 문장에는 X표를 하세요.

1 I had a nightmare about failing the test. (   )

2 They have opportunity to learn Chinese. (   )

3 The students took a part in the community cleanup event. (   )

4 I don't want to take class on painting. (   )

D 그림을 보고, 우리말 뜻에 맞게 문장을 완성해 보세요. (수 일치와 시제에 주의하세요.)

1 우리는 오해 때문에 싸웠다.

We _____ _____ _____ over a misunderstanding.

2 그녀는 시끄러운 소음 때문에 머리가 아프다.

She _____ _____ _____ from the loud noise.

3 그들은 공항에 제시간에 가기 위해 택시를 타야 했다.

They had to _____ _____ _____ to go to the airport on time.

4 수업 시간에 필기를 하는 것은 중요하다.

It is important to _____ _____ during the class.

do / make

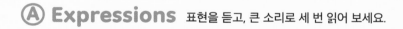

do [du] 통 하다, 이행하다, 다하다
did-done

Ⓐ Expressions 표현을 듣고, 큰 소리로 세 번 읽어 보세요.

MP3-005

❶

□ □ □

do one's best
최선을 다하다

❷

□ □ □

**do one's
homework**
숙제를 하다

❸

□ □ □

do a good job
훌륭하게 일을 해내다

❹

□ □ □

**do something
wrong**
무언가 잘못하다

❺

□ □ □

do one's duty
의무를[책임을] 다하다

❻

□ □ □

do one's chores 집안일을 하다

❼

□ □ □

do exercise
운동을 하다

❽

□ □ □

do the dishes
설거지를 하다

ⓑ Check the Expressions

문장을 듣고, 빈칸에 알맞은 단어를 써 보세요.

1 If you _____ _____ _____, you have a chance to succeed.

최선을 다하면 당신은 성공할 기회가 있다.

2 It is important to _____ _____ _____ by yourself.

너 스스로 숙제를 하는 것이 중요하다.

3 We work together to _____ _____ _____ _____ on this assignment.

우리는 이 과제를 잘 해내기 위해서 함께 일한다.

4 He knew he had _____ _____ _____.

그는 자신이 무언가 잘못했다는 것을 알았다.

5 Doctors need to _____ _____ _____ to care for the sick.

의사들은 환자들을 돌볼 의무를 다해야 한다.

6 I was taught by my parents to _____ _____ _____.

나는 부모님으로부터 내 몫의 집안일을 하도록 배웠다.

7 You should _____ _____ for 30 minutes a day.

너희는 하루에 30분씩 운동을 해야 한다.

8 It was my turn to _____ _____ _____.

내가 설거지를 할 차례였다.

⭐ It's my turn ~~doing~~ the dishes. (X)

Word Box | chore 몡 (집 청소 등의 정기적으로 하는) 일, 하기 싫은 일   assignment 몡 과제   turn 몡 차례

make [meik] 동 ~하게 하다, 만들다, 이루다
made-made

Ⓐ Expressions 표현을 듣고, 큰 소리로 세 번 읽어 보세요.

❶ ☐☐☐

make a point
주장을 밝히다

❷ ☐☐☐

make a speech
연설하다

❸ ☐☐☐

make a promise
약속하다

❹ ☐☐☐

make a mistake
실수하다

❺ ☐☐☐

make progress
진전을 보이다

❻ ☐☐☐

make up one's mind
마음을 결정하다, 결심하다

❼ ☐☐☐

make a difference
차별을 두다, 변화를 가져오다

❽ ☐☐☐

make a mess
엉망으로 만들다

Ⓑ Check the Expressions

문장을 듣고, 빈칸에 알맞은 단어를 써 보세요.

1 I'm trying to _____ _____ _____ about the power of art.

나는 예술이 가지는 힘에 대해 주장하려고 한다.

2 He is nervous when he _____ _____ _____.

그는 연설을 할 때 긴장을 한다.

3 I _____ _____ _____ to take care of my pet.

나는 내 반려동물을 돌보겠다고 약속했다.

4 Be careful not to _____ the same _____ again.

같은 실수를 반복하지 않도록 조심하세요.

⭐ He ~~did~~ a mistake. (X)

5 The students _____ great _____ in their English.

학생들은 영어 실력에서 상당한 진전을 보였다.

6 You'd better _____ _____ _____ _____ soon.

너는 빨리 마음을 결정하는 것이 좋겠다.

7 Our efforts can _____ _____ _____ in saving animals.

우리의 노력이 동물들을 살리는 데 변화를 가져올 수 있다.

8 They used to _____ _____ _____ in the house.

그들은 집안을 엉망으로 어지럽히곤 했다.

Word Box | progress 명 진전 동 진전을 보이다 effort 명 노력 save 동 구하다, 살리다 used to ~하곤 했다

A 다음 문장의 빈칸에 공통으로 들어가는 단어를 써 보세요.

1 If you _____ your best, you have a chance to succeed.

   We work together to _____ a good job on this assignment.

   ☐

2 I'm trying to _____ a point about the power of art.

   Be careful not to _____ the same mistake again.

   ☐

B <보기>에 주어진 단어를 이용하여 다음의 표현을 완성하세요.

> 보기
> do mistake something progress
> make wrong duty

1 무언가 잘못하다 _____ _____ _____

2 의무를 다하다 _____ one's _____

3 실수하다 _____ a _____

4 진전을 보이다 _____ _____

C 다음 중 옳은 표현이 사용된 문장에는 O, 그렇지 않은 문장에는 X표를 하세요.

1 I was told to do my chores. (　　)

2 It was my turn to do the dish. (　　)

3 You'd better make up your mind soon. (　　)

4 They used to make mess in the house. (　　)

D 그림을 보고, 우리말 뜻에 맞게 문장을 완성해 보세요. (수 일치와 시제에 주의하세요.)

1 너 스스로 숙제를 하는 것이 중요하다.

It is important to _____ your _____ by yourself.

2 너희는 하루에 30분씩 운동을 해야 한다.

You should _____ _____ for 30 minutes a day.

3 나는 연설을 할 때 긴장을 한다.

I am nervous when I _____ _____ _____.

4 나는 남동생을 잘 돌보겠다고 약속했다.

I _____ _____ _____ to take care of my brother.

break [breik] 동 깨다, 어기다, 부러지다, 알려지다
broke-broken

Ⓐ Expressions 표현을 듣고, 큰 소리로 세 번 읽어 보세요.

MP3-009

❶ ☐☐☐

break into pieces
산산조각이 나다

❷ ☐☐☐

break a law
법을 어기다

❸ ☐☐☐

break one's heart
마음을 아프게 하다

❹ ☐☐☐

break a record
기록을 깨다

❺ ☐☐☐

break down 고장 나다, 실패하다

❻ ☐☐☐

break out 발생하다, (전쟁 등이) 발발하다

❼ ☐☐☐

break the spell
(마법) 주문을 풀다

❽ ☐☐☐

break the news to
~에게 (좋지 않은) 소식을 전하다

Ⓑ Check the Expressions

문장을 듣고, 빈칸에 알맞은 단어를 써 보세요.

1 The vase fell off and _____ _____ _____.

꽃병이 떨어져서 산산조각이 났다.　　　⭐ The glass fell off and broke into ~~piece~~. (X)

2 If you _____ _____ _____, you will be punished.

법을 어기면 당신은 처벌을 받을 것이다.

3 Seeing the abandoned dogs _____ _____ _____.

유기견들을 보고 나는 마음이 아팠다.

4 The new blockbuster movie _____ _____ _____.

신작 블록버스터 영화가 기록을 깼다.

5 The car _____ _____ on the highway yesterday.

어제 고속도로에서 차가 고장 났다.

6 When the war _____ _____, they had to leave their homes.

전쟁이 났을 때, 그들은 집을 떠나야 했다.

7 The true love finally _____ _____ _____.

진정한 사랑이 마침내 마법을 풀었다.

8 He is going to _____ _____ _____ _____ his employees.

그는 직원들에게 유감스러운 소식을 전할 것이다.

Word Box | spell 몡 마법, 주문　punish 통 처벌하다　abandon 통 버리다, 유기하다　employee 몡 직원, 고용인

catch [kætʃ] 툉 잡다, (병에) 걸리다, (불이) 붙다
caught-caught

MP3-011

Ⓐ **Expressions** 표현을 듣고, 큰 소리로 세 번 읽어 보세요.

❶ □□□

catch a ball
공을 잡다

❷ □□□

EXHIBITION

catch one's eye
눈길을 사로잡다

❸ □□□

catch up (with)
(사람, 수준 등을) 따라잡다

❹ □□□

catch a cold
감기에 걸리다

❺ □□□

catch fire 불붙다

❻ □□□

catch one's attention
~의 관심을[주의를] 끌다

❼ □□□

catch one's breath
숨을 고르다

❽ □□□

catch someone later
나중에 보다[만나다]

ⒷCheck the Expressions

문장을 듣고, 빈칸에 알맞은 단어를 써 보세요.

MP3-012

1 The goalkeeper dived to _____ _____ _____.

골키퍼는 공을 잡기 위해 몸을 날렸다.

2 The ad _____ _____ _____ with its unique idea.

그 광고는 독특한 발상으로 내 이목을 끌었다.

⭐ It caught my eyes. (X)

3 I'm trying hard to _____ _____ _____ the others.

나는 다른 사람들을 따라가기 위해 열심히 노력하고 있다.

4 It's easy to _____ _____ _____ or flu in winter.

겨울엔 감기나 독감에 걸리기 쉽다.

5 The airplane _____ _____ and crashed.

그 비행기는 불이 나서 추락했다.

6 He made a joke to _____ students' _____.

그는 학생들의 주의를 끌기 위해 농담을 했다.

7 Please take a break and _____ _____ _____.

좀 쉬면서 숨을 돌리세요.

8 I'm busy right now, but I'll _____ _____ _____.

지금은 제가 바쁘니 나중에 봐요.

Word Box | attention 몡 주의, 흥미 unique 혱 독특한 ad 몡 광고(=advertisement)

A 다음 문장의 빈칸에 공통으로 들어가는 단어를 써 보세요.

1 I heard the car _____ down on the highway. (과거형)

He _____ the news to his employees. (과거형)

2 Please take a break and _____ your breath.

I'm busy right now, but I'll _____ you later.

B <보기>에 주어진 단어를 이용하여 다음의 표현을 완성하세요.

보기	break spell heart catch cold up

1 ~의 마음을 아프게 하다   _____ one's _____

2 마법을 풀다   _____ the _____

3 (사람, 수준을) 따라잡다   _____ _____ (with)

4 감기에 걸리다   _____ a _____

C 다음 중 옳은 표현이 사용된 문장에는 O, 그렇지 않은 문장에는 X표를 하세요.

1 The new film broke a record. (   )

2 When the war broke out, they had to leave their homes. (   )

3 The ad caught my eye with its bold color. (   )

4 I made a joke to caught students' attention. (   )

D 그림을 보고, 우리말 뜻에 맞게 문장을 완성해 보세요. (수 일치와 시제에 주의하세요.)

1 접시가 떨어져서 산산조각이 났다.

The dish fell off and _____ _____ _____.

2 법을 어기면 처벌을 받을 것이다.

If you _____ a _____, you will be punished.

3 그는 공을 잡으러 몸을 날렸다.

He dived to _____ a _____.

4 집에 불이 났을 때 그는 119에 전화했다.

He called 119 when the house _____ _____.

Unit 04 come / go

come [kʌm] 통 오다, 되다, 나오다, 가다, 생기다
came-come

Ⓐ Expressions 표현을 듣고, 큰 소리로 세 번 읽어 보세요.

❶ ☐ ☐ ☐

come from ~ 출신이다, ~에서 생겨나다

❷ ☐ ☐ ☐

come to an end 끝나다, 죽다

❸ ☐ ☐ ☐

come up with ~을 마련하다, 제시하다

❹ ☐ ☐ ☐

come to a conclusion 결론에 도달하다

❺ ☐ ☐ ☐

80%

come close 거의 ~할 뻔하다

❻ ☐ ☐ ☐

come along 도착하다, 함께 가다, 되어 가다

❼ ☐ ☐ ☐

come across 이해되다, (우연히) 찾다 [발견하다]

❽ ☐ ☐ ☐

come to think of it 그러고 보니, 생각해 보니

Ⓑ Check the Expressions

문장을 듣고, 빈칸에 알맞은 단어를 써 보세요.

1 Jason _____ _____ Chicago ten years ago.

제이슨은 10년 전에 시카고에서 왔다.

2 Their argument didn't _____ _____ _____ _____.

그들의 논쟁은 끝나지 않았다.

3 We couldn't _____ _____ _____ a better plan.

우리는 더 좋은 계획을 생각해 내지 못했다.

4 The scientists finally _____ _____ _____ _____ about the virus.

과학자들은 그 바이러스에 관해 마침내 결론에 도달했다.   ⭐ It went to a conclusion. (X)

5 I _____ so _____ to the finals.

나는 결승전에 거의 진출할 뻔했다.

6 Our project is starting to _____ _____ nicely.

우리 프로젝트는 잘 되어가기 시작하고 있다.

7 His point _____ _____ at his speech.

그의 이야기의 핵심은 연설에 잘 나타났다.

8 _____ _____ _____ _____ _____, I forgot to tell you something.

생각해 보니 너에게 잊고 말하지 않은 것이 있다.

Word Box | conclusion 몡 결론   virus 몡 바이러스   finals 몡 결승전

go [gou] 동 가다, 계속하다, ~에 달하다, 되어 가다
went-gone

Ⓐ Expressions 표현을 듣고, 큰 소리로 세 번 읽어 보세요.

❶

□ □ □
go abroad
해외로 가다

❷
□ □ □
go shopping
쇼핑하러 가다

❸
□ □ □
go on a picnic
소풍 가다

❹

□ □ □
go ahead
먼저 가다, 계속하다

❺

□ □ □
go bankrupt
파산하다

❻

□ □ □
go online
온라인에 접속하다

❼

□ □ □
go crazy 미치다, 열광하다

❽
□ □ □
go over something
~을 살펴보다, 검토하다

Ⓑ Check the Expressions

MP3-016

문장을 듣고, 빈칸에 알맞은 단어를 써 보세요.

1 I hope I can _____ _____ to study.

나는 외국에 유학 갈 수 있기를 희망한다.

2 I _____ _____ for my friend's present.

나는 친구의 선물을 사기 위해 쇼핑하러 갔다.

3 We _____ _____ _____ _____ last weekend.

우리는 지난 주말에 소풍을 갔다.

4 Jisoo decided to _____ _____ with her dream.

지수는 자신의 꿈을 계속 지켜 가기로 결심했다.

5 The company may _____ _____ in the near future.

그 회사는 가까운 미래에 파산할 수도 있다.   ⭐ They will go ~~to~~ bankrupt. (X)

6 During the pandemic, schools had to _____ _____.

팬데믹 기간 동안 학교들은 온라인으로 접속해야 했다.

7 Teenagers _____ _____ over hip-hop.

십 대들은 힙합에 열광한다.

8 You need to _____ _____ your writing again.

너는 네 작문을 다시 검토해 볼 필요가 있다.

Word Box | bankrupt 형 파산한 동 파산시키다   pandemic 명 세계적인 유행병

A 다음 문장의 빈칸에 공통으로 들어가는 단어를 써 보세요.

1   Our project is starting to _____ along nicely.

Her point will _____ across at her presentation.

2   I hope I can _____ abroad to study someday.

He decided to _____ ahead with his plan.

B <보기>에 주어진 단어를 이용하여 다음의 표현을 완성하세요.

보기   come   crazy   from   close   over   go

1   ~에서 오다, 출신이다   _____ _____

2   거의 ~할 뻔하다   _____ _____

3   열광하다   _____ _____

4   검토하다   _____ _____

C 다음 중 옳은 표현이 사용된 문장에는 O, 그렇지 않은 문장에는 X표를 하세요.

1 The teachers finally came to conclusion about it. (   )

2 We couldn't come up a better idea. (   )

3 We went on a picnic last month. (   )

4 They may go to bankrupt in the near future. (   )

D 그림을 보고, 우리말 뜻에 맞게 문장을 완성해 보세요. (수 일치와 시제에 주의하세요.)

1 그들의 논쟁은 끝나지 않았다.

Their argument didn't _____ _____ an _____.

2 생각해 보니 너에게 잊고 말하지 않은 것이 있다.

_____ _____ _____ _____ _____, I forgot to tell you something.

3 나는 부모님의 선물을 사기 위해 쇼핑을 갔다.

I _____ _____ for my parents' present.

4 팬데믹 기간 동안 학교들은 온라인으로 접속해야 했다.

During the pandemic, schools had to _____ _____.

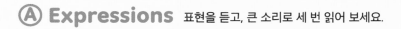

get [get] 통 얻다, 받다, (~의 상태가) 되다
got-gotten

Ⓐ Expressions 표현을 듣고, 큰 소리로 세 번 읽어 보세요.

MP3-017

❶ ☐ ☐ ☐

get a chance
기회를 얻다

❷ ☐ ☐ ☐

get a clue
단서를 얻다

❸ ☐ ☐ ☐

get fired
해고되다

❹ ☐ ☐ ☐

get tired of
~에 질리다, 싫증이 나다

❺ ☐ ☐ ☐

get together
모이다, 정리하다

❻ ☐ ☐ ☐

get dressed
옷을 입다

❼ ☐ ☐ ☐

get pregnant
임신하다

❽ ☐ ☐ ☐

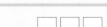

get hurt
다치다

Ⓑ Check the Expressions

MP3-018

문장을 듣고, 빈칸에 알맞은 단어를 써 보세요.

1 If I _____ _____ _____, I'll do my best.

기회를 얻는다면 나는 최선을 다할 것이다.

2 The detective _____ _____ _____ about the accident.

형사는 그 사건에 대한 단서를 얻었다.

3 Many people _____ _____ over the budget cuts.

많은 사람들이 예산 삭감으로 인해 해고되었다.

4 Kelly _____ _____ _____ listening to their complaints.

켈리는 그들의 불평을 들어주는 데 지쳤다.

5 We should _____ _____ sometime.

우리 언제 한번 만나자.

6 They couldn't _____ _____ by themselves.

그들은 혼자 옷을 입을 수 없었다.

7 Elephants _____ _____ for about 22 months.

코끼리는 약 22개월 동안 임신한다.

⭐ She ~~did~~ pregnant. (X)

8 Luckily no one _____ _____ during the fire.

다행스럽게도 화재 당시 아무도 다치지 않았다.

Word Box detective 몡 형사, 탐정   budget 몡 예산   cut 몡 삭감, 인하   complaint 몡 불평, 항의

keep [ki:p] 동 유지하다, 계속하다, ~인 상태를 지키다, 막다
kept-kept

(A) Expressions 표현을 듣고, 큰 소리로 세 번 읽어 보세요.

MP3-019

❶
keep quiet
조용히 하다, 비밀로 해 두다

❷
keep a diary
일기를 쓰다

❸
keep a secret
비밀을 지키다

❹
keep calm
침착하다, 평정을 유지하다

❺
keep in touch
계속 연락하다

❻
keep up with 유행을 따르다, ~에 뒤지지 않다

❼
keep an eye on
~을 지켜보다, 감시하다

❽
keep one's distance
거리를 두다

ⓑ Check the Expressions

문장을 듣고, 빈칸에 알맞은 단어를 써 보세요.

1 Students must _____ _____ in the library.

학생들은 도서관에서 조용히 해야 한다.

2 _____ _____ _____ helps me practice writing.

일기를 쓰는 것은 내가 작문 연습을 하는 데 도움이 된다.

3 I promised to _____ _____ _____ with him.

나는 그와 비밀을 지키겠다고 약속했다.

4 It's hard to _____ _____ in this stressful situation.

이렇게 스트레스 받는 상황에서는 평정을 유지하기 힘들다.

5 I hope I can _____ _____ _____ with you.

너와 계속 연락하고 지낼 수 있으면 좋겠다.

6 They couldn't _____ _____ _____ all the changes.

그들은 그 모든 변화를 따라갈 수가 없었다.

7 Would you _____ _____ _____ _____ my backpack?

제 책가방 좀 봐 주시겠어요?

8 _____ _____ _____ from people who are coughing.

기침하는 사람들과 거리를 두세요.
⭐ ~~Make~~ your distance from people. (X)

Word Box distance 명 거리 stressful 형 스트레스가 많은 cough 동 기침하다 명 기침

A 다음 문장의 빈칸에 공통으로 들어가는 단어를 써 보세요.

1 If I _____ a chance, I'll do my best.

You'll _____ a clue about the mystery.

2 It's hard to _____ calm when you're upset.

Please _____ your distance from strangers.

B <보기>에 주어진 단어를 이용하여 다음의 표현을 완성하세요.

보기	keep dressed secret up get with pregnant

1 옷을 입다 _____ _____

2 임신하다 _____ _____

3 비밀을 지키다 _____ a _____

4 유행을 따르다 _____ _____ _____

C 다음 중 옳은 표현이 사용된 문장에는 O, 그렇지 않은 문장에는 X표를 하세요.

1 If you don't work hard, you will get fired. (　　)

2 I got tired of listening to the same song. (　　)

3 I hope I can keep touch with you. (　　)

4 Will you keep an eye on my bag? (　　)

D 그림을 보고, 우리말 뜻에 맞게 문장을 완성해 보세요. (수 일치와 시제에 주의하세요.)

1 우리는 오늘 오후에 만나야 한다.

We should _____ _____ this afternoon.

2 운동장에서 다치지 않게 조심해라.

Be careful not to _____ _____ on the playground.

3 사람들은 도서관에서 조용히 해야 한다.

People must _____ _____ in the library.

4 나는 오랫동안 일기를 써 왔다.

I have _____ _____ _____ for a long time.

give [giv] 통 주다, 전하다, 제공하다, 기부하다
gave-given

Ⓐ Expressions 표현을 듣고, 큰 소리로 세 번 읽어 보세요.

MP3-021

❶

give up
포기하다

❷
give an
example
예를 들다

❸
give an opinion 의견을 말하다

❹

give someone
directions
~에게 길을 알려주다

❺

give permission
허가를 주다

❻

give an
impression
인상을 주다

❼

give away
저버리다, 양보하다

❽

give someone
a break
~를 너그럽게 봐주다,
내버려두다

Ⓑ Check the Expressions

문장을 듣고, 빈칸에 알맞은 단어를 써 보세요.

1 I would not _____ _____ on any dream.

나는 어떤 꿈도 포기하지 않을 것이다.

2 Would you _____ _____ _____ of a passive sentence?

수동태 문장의 예를 하나 들어주시겠어요?

3 We are not ready to _____ _____ _____ on it.

우리는 그것에 관해 의견을 말할 준비가 되지 않다.

4 A kind lady _____ _____ _____ to the store.

친절한 아주머니께서 나에게 가게로 가는 길을 알려 주셨다.

5 The teacher _____ _____ to leave early.

선생님께서 조퇴하는 것을 허락해 주셨다.

6 New volunteers _____ us _____ good _____.

새로운 자원봉사자들은 우리에게 좋은 인상을 주었다.   ⭐ He ~~showed~~ a good impression. (X)

7 She had to _____ _____ a good opportunity.

그녀는 좋은 기회를 양보해야 했다.

8 I hope she could _____ _____ _____ _____ for a while.

나는 그녀가 잠시라도 내게 쉴 틈을 주면 좋겠다.

> **Word Box** | permission 몡 허락, 승인   impression 몡 인상, 감명   passive 몡 수동태 몡 수동적인

save [seiv] 통 구하다, 절약하다, 저축하다, 챙겨 두다, 면하게 하다

Ⓐ Expressions 표현을 듣고, 큰 소리로 세 번 읽어 보세요.

MP3-023

❶ □□□
save time
시간을 절약하다

❷ □□□
save energy
에너지를 절약하다

❸ □□□
save one's life
~의 목숨을 구하다

❹ □□□
save space
공간을 절약하다

❺ □□□
save money
돈을 모으다

❻ □□□
save a seat
자리를 맡다

❼ □□□
save a file
파일을 저장하다

❽ □□□
save someone trouble
~의 수고를 덜어 주다

Ⓑ Check the Expressions

문장을 듣고, 빈칸에 알맞은 단어를 써 보세요.

MP3-024

1 They took a shortcut to _____ _____.

그들은 시간을 절약하기 위해 지름길로 갔다.　　⭐ **You can save** ~~many~~ **time.** (X) **a lot of time** (O)

2 Using public transportation can _____ _____.

대중교통을 이용하는 것으로 에너지를 절약할 수 있다.

3 The lifeguard _____ _____ _____ in the sea.

인명 구조원이 바다에서 내 목숨을 구했다.

4 I organized my files to _____ _____.

나는 공간을 절약하기 위해 내 파일들을 정리했다.

5 I wish I had _____ more _____.

돈을 좀 더 모았으면 좋았을 텐데.

6 Jason always _____ _____ _____ for his friend.

제이슨은 항상 친구의 자리를 맡아 준다.

7 Don't forget to _____ _____ _____ after making changes.

수정한 후에 파일을 저장하는 것을 잊지 마세요.

8 Planning ahead can _____ _____ a lot of _____.

미리 계획을 하는 것으로 너는 많은 수고를 덜 수 있다.

Word Box | shortcut 몡 지름길　public 혱 공공의, 대중의　lifeguard 몡 인명 구조원　organize 동 정리하다

A   다음 문장의 빈칸에 공통으로 들어가는 단어를 써 보세요.

1   I would not _____ up on any dream.

She had to _____ away a good opportunity.

2   I organized my files to _____ space.

Planning ahead can _____ you a lot of troble.

B   <보기>에 주어진 단어를 이용하여 다음의 표현을 완성하세요.

보기	give file impression energy break save

1   인상을 주다   _____ an _____

2   ~를 너그럽게 봐주다,   _____ someone a _____
내버려두다

3   에너지를 아끼다   _____ _____

4   파일을 저장하다   _____ a _____

C 다음 중 옳은 표현이 사용된 문장에는 O, 그렇지 않은 문장에는 X표를 하세요.

1 Could you give example of your answer? (　　)

2 I'm not ready to give an opinion on it. (　　)

3 He always saves seat for his friend. (　　)

4 The lifeguard saved me life in the sea. (　　)

D 그림을 보고, 우리말 뜻에 맞게 문장을 완성해 보세요. (수 일치와 시제에 주의하세요.)

1
그는 나에게 쇼핑몰로 가는 길을 알려 주었다.

He _____ _____ _____ to the shopping mall.

2
그녀의 엄마는 그녀에게 여행을 가도 좋다고 허락했다.

Her mother _____ _____ for her to go on a trip.

3
우리는 시간을 절약하기 위해 비행기를 탔다.

We took an airplane to _____ _____.

4
미래를 위해 돈을 절약하는 것이 좋다.

You'd better _____ _____ for the future.

Expression Check List

→ 아는 표현 앞에 √ 표시를 해 보세요. 기억나지 않는 표현은 다시 확인해 암기하세요.

√	표현	√	표현	√	표현
	have a chat		do the dishes		catch one's breath
	have a fight		make a point		catch someone later
	have a headache		make a speech		
	have a nightmare		make a promise		
	have an argument		make a mistake		
	have an effect (on)		make progress		
	have an experience		make up one's mind		
	have an opportunity		make a difference		
	take a class		make a mess		
	take an exam		break into pieces		
	take advantage of		break a law		
	take a taxi		break one's heart		
	take notes		break a record		
	take a risk		break down		
	take part (in)		break out		
	take place		break the spell		
	do one's best		break the news to		
	do one's homework		catch a ball		
	do a good job		catch one's eye		
	do something wrong		catch up (with)		
	do one's duty		catch a cold		
	do one's chores		catch fire		
	do exercise		catch one's attention		

Unit 01~03

알고 있는 표현 수 [   ]

다시 암기할 표현 수 [   ]

√	표현	√	표현	√	표현
	come from		get hurt		save a file
	come to an end		keep quiet		save someone trouble
	come up with		keep a diary		
	come to a conclusion		keep a secret		
	come close		keep calm		
	come along		keep in touch		
	come across		keep up with		
	come to think of it		keep an eye on		
	go abroad		keep one's distance		
	go shopping		give up		
	go on a picnic		give an example		
	go ahead		give an opinion		
	go bankrupt		give someone directions		
	go online		give permission		
	go crazy		give an impression		
	go over something		give away		
	get a chance		give someone a break		
	get a clue		save time		
	get fired		save energy		
	get tired of		save one's life		
	get together		save space		
	get dressed		save money		
	get pregnant		save a seat		

Unit 04~06

알고 있는 표현 수

다시 암기할 표현 수

Chapter 2

빈출동사와
영어표현

Ⓐ Expressions 표현을 듣고, 큰 소리로 세 번씩 읽어 보세요.

MP3-025

arrive
[əráiv] 통 도착하다, 도래하다, 도달하다

WELCOME HOME!

❶ **arrive home**
집에 도착하다

❷ **arrive on time**
정각에 도착하다

❸ **arrive shortly**
곧 도착하다

❹ **arrive late**
늦게 도착하다

answer
[ǽnsər] 통 대답하다, 응답하다
명 대답, 해답, 응답

❶ **answer the question**
질문에 답하다

❷ **answer the phone**
전화를 받다

❸ **give someone an answer**
~에게 대답을 해 주다

❹ **wait for an answer**
답을 기다리다

Ⓑ Check the Expressions

문장을 듣고, 빈칸에 알맞은 단어를 써 보세요.

 MP3-026

arrive

1 I usually _____ _____ around 5 p.m. after school.

나는 주로 방과 후 5시쯤 집에 도착한다.   ⭐ I arrive ~~to~~ home. (X)

2 All the students had _____ _____ _____ for the class.

모든 학생들이 수업에 맞추어 정각에 도착했다.

3 She would _____ _____ for the group meeting.

그녀는 모둠 회의에 곧 도착할 것이다.

4 I _____ _____ to the cinema last night.

나는 어젯밤 영화관에 늦게 도착했다.

answer

1 You'd better think carefully before _____ _____ _____.

질문에 답하기 전에 곰곰이 생각해 보는 것이 좋겠다.

2 Could somebody _____ _____ _____, please?

누가 전화 좀 받아 주시겠어요?

3 I'll _____ _____ _____ _____ tomorrow.

내가 내일 너에게 대답을 해 줄게.

4 We're _____ _____ _____ _____ from the board.

우리는 위원회의 대답을 기다리고 있다.

Word Box | shortly 🄫 곧   carefully 🄫 조심스럽게, 세심하게   board 🄼 위원회, 이사회

Unit 01 arrive / answer / ask / believe

Ⓐ Expressions 표현을 듣고, 큰 소리로 세 번씩 읽어 보세요.

MP3-027

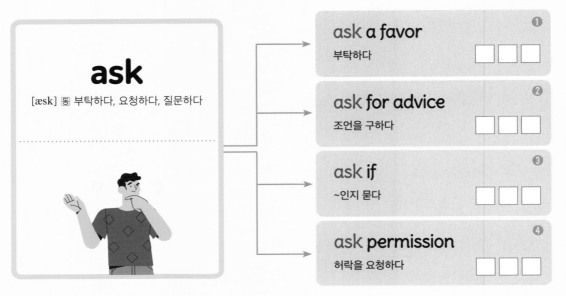

ask
[æsk] 동 부탁하다, 요청하다, 질문하다

❶ ask a favor
부탁하다 ☐ ☐ ☐

❷ ask for advice
조언을 구하다 ☐ ☐ ☐

❸ ask if
~인지 묻다 ☐ ☐ ☐

❹ ask permission
허락을 요청하다 ☐ ☐ ☐

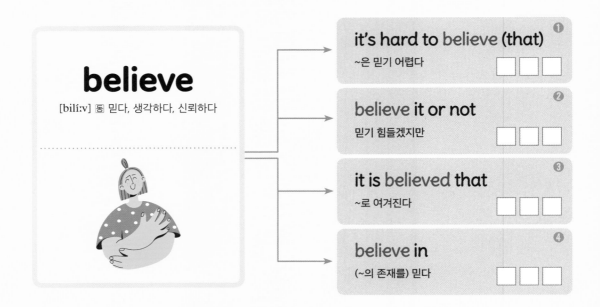

believe
[bilíːv] 동 믿다, 생각하다, 신뢰하다

❶ it's hard to believe (that)
~은 믿기 어렵다 ☐ ☐ ☐

❷ believe it or not
믿기 힘들겠지만 ☐ ☐ ☐

❸ it is believed that
~로 여겨진다 ☐ ☐ ☐

❹ believe in
(~의 존재를) 믿다 ☐ ☐ ☐

ⒷCheck the Expressions

문장을 듣고, 빈칸에 알맞은 단어를 써 보세요.

MP3-028

ask

1 I need to _____ _____ _____ of you.

너에게 부탁할 것이 있어.

⭐ They asked ~~to~~ me for a favor. (X)

2 She _____ _____ _____ on writing a story.

그녀는 이야기를 쓰는 것에 대해 조언을 구했다.

3 Minho _____ _____ he could borrow my laptop.

민호는 내 노트북을 빌릴 수 있는지 물었다.

4 We _____ _____ to leave the class early.

우리는 조퇴하는 것에 허락을 구했다.

believe

1 _____ _____ _____ _____ _____ the city used to be small.

그 도시가 작았었다는 것은 믿기 어렵다.

2 _____ _____ _____ _____, I have never gone to the dentist.

믿기 힘들겠지만 나는 치과에 가본 적이 없다.

3 _____ _____ _____ _____ dolphins are very intelligent.

돌고래들은 지능이 매우 높다고 알려져 있다.

4 I always _____ _____ the power of positive thinking.

나는 항상 긍정적인 생각의 힘을 믿는다.

Word Box | favor 몡 부탁, 호의   intelligent 혱 총명한, 똑똑한, 지능이 있는

A 우리말 뜻에 맞게 단어들을 연결하세요.

1 정각에 도착하다   arrive   •   • an answer

2 대답을 기다리다   wait for   •   • or not

3 믿기 힘들겠지만   believe it   •   • on time

4 부탁하다   ask   •   • a favor

B <보기>에 주어진 단어를 이용하여 우리말 뜻에 맞게 문장을 완성해 보세요. (수 일치와 시제에 주의하세요.)

보기
      arrive   ask   answer   believe

1 I'll give you an _____ tomorrow.
   내가 내일 대답을 해 줄 것이다.

2 I always _____ in the power of positive thinking.
   나는 항상 긍정적인 생각의 힘을 믿는다.

3 Minho _____ if he could borrow my laptop.
   민호는 내 노트북을 빌릴 수 있는지 물었다.

4 She would _____ shortly for the group meeting.
   그녀는 모둠 회의에 곧 도착할 것이다.

다음 문장의 빈칸에 공통으로 들어가는 단어를 써 보세요.

1 They would _____ on time.

   We should not _____ late for the flight.

   ┌─────────────────┐
   │   │
   └─────────────────┘

2 The teacher will _____ the questions from students.

   Would you _____ the phone for me?

   ┌─────────────────┐
   │   │
   └─────────────────┘

D 다음 중 옳은 표현이 쓰인 문장을 고르세요.

1 ① He arrived to home.

   ② He arrived home.

2 ① They are waiting for answer from him.

   ② They are waiting for an answer from him.

3 ① I asked for advice on how to create my blog.

   ② I asked for an advice on how to create my blog.

4 ① It is believe that whales are very intelligent.

   ② It is believed that whales are very intelligent.

bring / call / cause / change

Ⓐ **Expressions** 표현을 듣고, 큰 소리로 세 번씩 읽어 보세요.

MP3-029

bring
broght - broght
[briŋ] 图 가져오다, 데려오다, 일으키다

❶ **bring peace**
평화를 가져오다 ☐☐☐

❷ **bring chaos**
혼돈을 가져오다 ☐☐☐

❸ **bring it to an end**
끝내다 ☐☐☐

❹ **bring someone joy**
~에게 기쁨을 주다 ☐☐☐

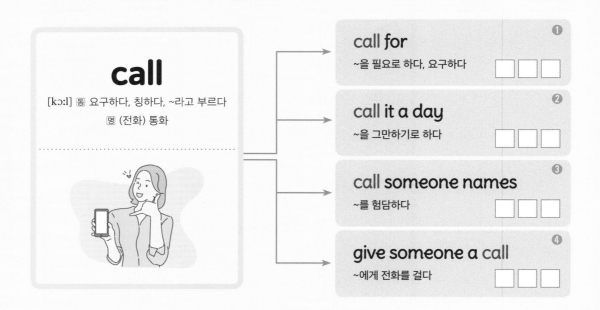

call
[kɔːl] 图 요구하다, 칭하다, ~라고 부르다
图 (전화) 통화

❶ **call for**
~을 필요로 하다, 요구하다 ☐☐☐

❷ **call it a day**
~을 그만하기로 하다 ☐☐☐

❸ **call someone names**
~를 험담하다 ☐☐☐

❹ **give someone a call**
~에게 전화를 걸다 ☐☐☐

Ⓑ Check the Expressions

문장을 듣고, 빈칸에 알맞은 단어를 써 보세요.

MP3-030

bring

1 It could _____ _____ to the world.

그것이 세계에 평화를 가져올 수 있다.

2 The sudden change _____ _____ to us.

갑작스러운 변화는 우리에게 혼돈을 가져왔다.

3 They need to _____ _____ _____ _____ _____ soon.

그들은 빨리 끝내야 한다.

4 Your presents _____ _____ great _____.

너희들의 선물은 나에게 큰 기쁨을 주었다.

call

1 The children _____ _____ help from their parents.

아이들이 자기 부모님에게 도움을 요청했다.

2 Let's _____ _____ _____ _____ and take a rest.

그만하고 쉬자.

3 They _____ _____ _____ but I ignored them.

그들이 나를 험담했지만 나는 그들을 무시했다.

4 Could you _____ _____ _____ _____ tomorrow?

내일 나한테 전화해 주시겠어요?

⭐ Please call ~~to~~ me tomorrow. (X)

Word Box | chaos 몡 혼돈   sudden 톙 갑작스러운   ignore 통 무시하다

Ⓐ **Expressions** 표현을 듣고, 큰 소리로 세 번씩 읽어 보세요.

MP3-031

cause

[kɔːz] 동 ~을 야기하다, 원인이 되다

EARTH

❶ **cause damage**
해를 끼치다

❷ **cause a disease**
질병을 유발하다

❸ **cause death**
죽게 하다

❹ **cause delay**
지연을 일으키다

change

[tʃeindʒ] 동 변하다, 변화시키다, 바꾸다

❶ **change one's mind**
~의 마음을 바꾸다

❷ **change into**
~로 변하다

❸ **change the situation**
상황을 바꾸다

❹ **change one's attitude**
~의 태도를 바꾸다

ⓑ Check the Expressions

문장을 듣고, 빈칸에 알맞은 단어를 써 보세요.

cause

1 The heavy snow _____ serious _____ to the roof.

폭설로 지붕에 심각한 손상이 생겼다.

2 We are trying to find out what _____ the _____.

우리는 무엇이 그 질병을 유발하는지 알아내기 위해 노력하고 있다.

3 Drinking and driving can _____ _____.

음주 운전은 목숨을 앗아갈 수 있다.

4 The storm _____ _____ at the airport.

폭풍으로 인해 공항에서 지연이 발생했다.

change

1 No matter what happens, I won't _____ _____ _____.

어떤 일이 생기더라도 나는 내 마음을 바꾸지 않을 것이다.

2 The frog _____ _____ a handsome prince.

개구리는 잘생긴 왕자님으로 변했다.

3 We can do anything to _____ _____ _____.

우리는 상황을 변화시키기 위해 어떤 일도 할 수 있다.

4 Why don't you _____ _____ _____ toward him?

그에 대한 당신의 태도를 바꾸는 게 어떨까요?

Word Box │ damage 몡 손상, 손해 attitude 몡 태도 no matter 상관없다, 괜찮다

A 우리말 뜻에 맞게 단어들을 연결하세요.

1	평화를 가져오다	bring •		• peace
2	~을 요구하다, 필요로 하다	call •		• delay
3	지연을 일으키다	cause •		• for
4	~의 태도를 바꾸다	change •		• one's attitude

B <보기>에 주어진 단어를 이용하여 우리말 뜻에 맞게 문장을 완성해 보세요. (수 일치와 시제에 주의하세요.)

보기	bring change cause call

1 The sudden change _____ chaos to us.

갑작스러운 변화는 우리에게 혼돈을 가져왔다.

2 They _____ me names but I ignored them.

그들이 나를 험담했지만 나는 그들을 무시했다.

3 Drinking and driving can _____ death.

음주 운전은 목숨을 앗아갈 수 있다.

4 No matter what happens, I won't _____ my mind.

어떤 일이 생기더라도 나는 내 마음을 바꾸지 않을 것이다.

다음 문장의 빈칸에 공통으로 들어가는 단어를 써 보세요.

1   The children will _____ for help from their teachers.

    Let's _____ it a day and go home.

2   I would never _____ my mind.

    We can do it to _____ the situation.

D   다음 중 옳은 표현이 쓰인 문장을 고르세요.

1   ① Please give to me a call next week.

    ② Please give me a call next week.

2   ① You need to bring it to an end now.

    ② You need to bring it to end now.

3   ① The storm cause damages to the fence.

    ② The storm caused damage to the fence.

4   ① The witch changed to a pretty princess.

    ② The witch changed into a pretty princess.

Ⓐ Expressions 표현을 듣고, 큰 소리로 세 번씩 읽어 보세요.

MP3-033

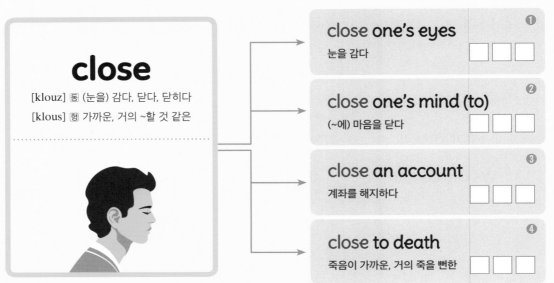

close

[klouz] 통 (눈을) 감다, 닫다, 닫히다
[klous] 형 가까운, 거의 ~할 것 같은

❶ close one's eyes
눈을 감다

❷ close one's mind (to)
(~에) 마음을 닫다

❸ close an account
계좌를 해지하다

❹ close to death
죽음이 가까운, 거의 죽을 뻔한

control

[kəntróul] 통 조절하다, 제어하다, 지배하다
명 지배, 통제

❶ control oneself
자신을 조절하다, 자제하다

❷ lose control of
~에 대한 통제력을 잃다

❸ under control
통제되는

❹ remote control
원격 조종, 리모컨

Ⓑ Check the Expressions

문장을 듣고, 빈칸에 알맞은 단어를 써 보세요.

close

1 I _____ _____ _____ and relaxed.

나는 눈을 감고 긴장을 풀었다.

2 I _____ _____ _____ _____ the possibility.

나는 그 가능성에 마음을 닫았다.

3 She _____ _____ _____ at the bank.

그녀는 은행에서 계좌를 해지했다.

4 The patient was _____ _____ _____.

그 환자는 거의 죽기 직전이었다.

control

1 You'd better learn how to _____ _____.

너는 자신을 어떻게 조절해야 하는지 배워야 한다.

2 The king _____ _____ _____ his kingdom.

왕은 자신의 왕국에 대한 통제력을 잃었다.

3 Don't worry. Everything is _____ _____.

걱정 마세요. 모든 일이 잘되고 있어요.　★ The situation is now under ~~the~~ control. (X)

4 We used to fight over the _____ _____.

우리는 서로 리모컨을 가지겠다고 싸우곤 했다.

Word Box | account 몡 계좌, 장부　remote 혱 먼, 원격의　possibility 몡 가능성　kingdom 몡 왕국

Ⓐ Expressions 표현을 듣고, 큰 소리로 세 번씩 읽어 보세요.

MP3-035

cook

[kuk] 통 요리하다
명 요리사

❶ cook **a meal**
식사 준비를 하다 ☐☐☐

❷ cook **something for dinner** 저녁으로
~을 만들다 ☐☐☐

❸ cook **breakfast**
아침을 만들다 ☐☐☐

❹ cook **something evenly**
~을 골고루 익히다 ☐☐☐

cut

cut - cut
[kʌt]] 통 자르다, 베다

❶ cut **along**
~을 따라 자르다 ☐☐☐

❷ cut **the lawn**
잔디를 깎다 ☐☐☐

❸ cut **one's finger**
손가락을 베다 ☐☐☐

❹ get **one's hair** cut
머리카락을 자르다 ☐☐☐

Ⓑ Check the Expressions

문장을 듣고, 빈칸에 알맞은 단어를 써 보세요.

cook

1 We _____ _____ _____ together while camping.

우리는 캠핑하면서 함께 식사 준비를 했다.

2 My mom _____ the fried rice _____ _____.

우리 엄마는 저녁으로 볶음밥을 하셨다.

3 My father was _____ _____ in the kitchen.

우리 아빠는 부엌에서 아침을 만들고 계셨다.

4 Turn the pancake to _____ _____ _____.

골고루 익게 팬케이크를 뒤집어라. ⭐ Mr. Lee is a very good ~~cooker.~~ (X) a very good cook (O)

cut

1 _____ _____ the dotted line and open it.

점선을 따라 자른 후 열어 보세요.

2 He spent the afternoon _____ _____ _____.

그는 잔디를 깎으며 오후 시간을 보냈다.

3 I _____ _____ _____ while opening the box.

나는 상자를 열다가 손가락을 베었다.

4 I went to the salon to _____ _____ _____ _____.

나는 머리를 자르기 위해 미용실에 갔다.

Word Box | evenly ⣿ 고르게, 균등하게   dotted line ⣿ 점선   salon ⣿ (미용실 등의) 상점

A 우리말 뜻에 맞게 단어들을 연결하세요.

1 계좌를 해지하다   close   •   •   the lawn

2 자신을 조절하다   control   •   •   an account

3 식사를 준비하다   cook   •   •   a meal

4 잔디를 깎다   cut   •   •   oneself

B <보기>에 주어진 단어를 이용하여 우리말 뜻에 맞게 문장을 완성해 보세요. (수 일치와 시제에 주의하세요.)

보기	cut close cook control

1 I _____ my mind to the possibility.

나는 그 가능성에 마음을 닫았다.

2 We used to fight over the remote _____.

우리는 서로 리모컨을 가지겠다고 싸우곤 했다.

3 Turn the pancake to _____ it evenly.

골고루 익게 팬케이크를 뒤집어라.

4 I went to the salon to get my hair _____.

나는 머리를 자르기 위해 미용실에 갔다.

C 다음 문장의 빈칸에 공통으로 들어가는 단어를 써 보세요.

1 I'm learning how to _____ myself.

Don't worry. Everything is under _____.

[ ]

2 We _____ a meal together every Sunday.

I _____ breakfast for my family.

[ ]

D 다음 중 옳은 표현이 쓰인 문장을 고르세요.

1 ① The patient was almost closed to death.

② The patient was almost close to death.

2 ① He lost a control of his company.

② He lost control of his company.

3 ① She cooked eggs for dinner.

② She cooked eggs to dinner.

4 ① Cut along with the dotted lines.

② Cut along the dotted lines.

Ⓐ Expressions 표현을 듣고, 큰 소리로 세 번씩 읽어 보세요.

MP3-037

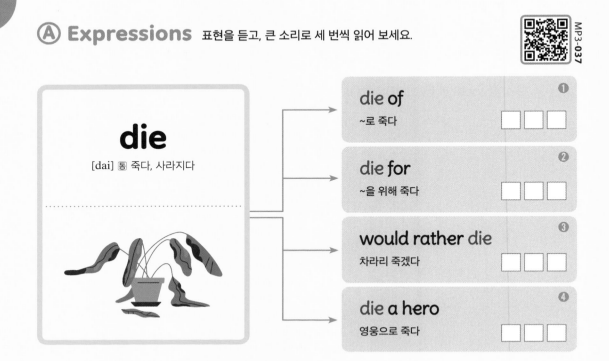

die

[dai] 동 죽다, 사라지다

❶ die of
~로 죽다

❷ die for
~을 위해 죽다

❸ would rather die
차라리 죽겠다

❹ die a hero
영웅으로 죽다

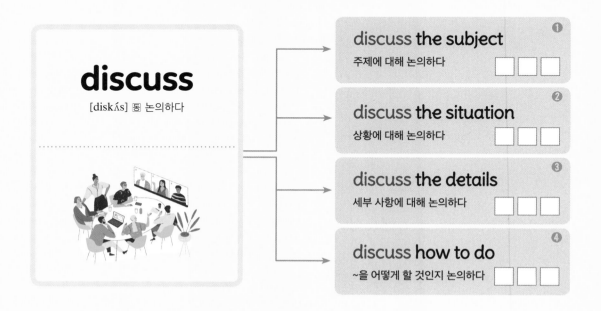

discuss

[diskʌs] 동 논의하다

❶ discuss the subject
주제에 대해 논의하다

❷ discuss the situation
상황에 대해 논의하다

❸ discuss the details
세부 사항에 대해 논의하다

❹ discuss how to do
~을 어떻게 할 것인지 논의하다

ⓑ Check the Expressions

문장을 듣고, 빈칸에 알맞은 단어를 써 보세요.

 MP3-038

die

1 The king _____ _____ a heart attack.

왕은 심장마비로 사망했다.

2 They fought and _____ _____ their freedom.

그들은 자유를 위해 싸웠고 목숨을 잃었다.

3 The soldiers _____ _____ _____ than surrender.

그 군인들은 항복을 하느니 차라리 죽을 것이다.

4 General Lee _____ _____ _____ in the battle.

이 장군은 그 전투에서 영웅으로 죽었다.

discuss

1 We set up a date to _____ _____ _____.

우리는 그 주제에 관해 논의하기 위해 날을 잡았다.

2 They _____ _____ _____ and made decisions.

그들은 상황을 논의하고 결정을 내렸다.

3 Let's get together to _____ _____ _____.

모여서 세부 사항을 논의하도록 하자.

⭐ We discuss ~~about~~ the details. (X)

4 They will _____ _____ _____ _____ this assignment.

그들은 이 과제를 어떻게 할지 논의할 것이다.

Word Box | rather 분 오히려, 차라리, 꽤   subject 명 주제, 학과, 과목   surrender 동 항복하다 명 항복

Ⓐ Expressions 표현을 듣고, 큰 소리로 세 번씩 읽어 보세요.

MP3-039

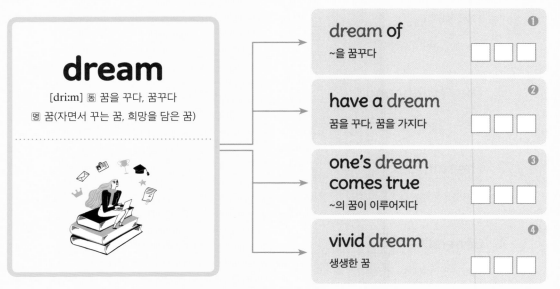

dream

[dri:m] 통 꿈을 꾸다, 꿈꾸다
명 꿈(자면서 꾸는 꿈, 희망을 담은 꿈)

❶ **dream of**
~을 꿈꾸다

❷ **have a dream**
꿈을 꾸다, 꿈을 가지다

❸ **one's dream comes true**
~의 꿈이 이루어지다

❹ **vivid dream**
생생한 꿈

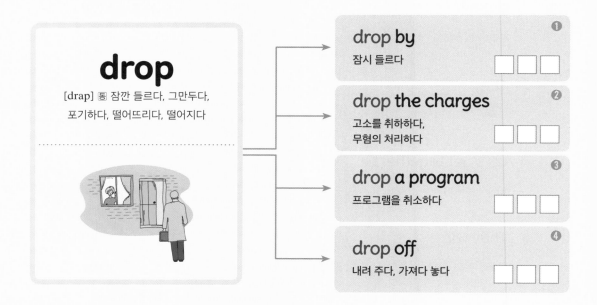

drop

[drap] 통 잠깐 들르다, 그만두다,
포기하다, 떨어뜨리다, 떨어지다

❶ **drop by**
잠시 들르다

❷ **drop the charges**
고소를 취하하다,
무혐의 처리하다

❸ **drop a program**
프로그램을 취소하다

❹ **drop off**
내려 주다, 가져다 놓다

Ⓑ Check the Expressions

문장을 듣고, 빈칸에 알맞은 단어를 써 보세요.

MP3-040

dream

1 I have _____ _____ becoming a doctor.

나는 의사가 되고 싶은 꿈을 꿔왔다.

★ I've dreamed ~~to be~~ a doctor. (X)

2 When I was a child, I _____ _____ wonderful _____.

어렸을 때, 나는 멋진 꿈이 있었다.

3 Her _____ finally _____ _____ after hard work.

고된 노력 끝에 그녀의 꿈이 마침내 이루어졌다.

4 I dreamed a _____ _____ last night.

나는 어젯밤 생생한 꿈을 꾸었다.

drop

1 I just _____ _____ to see if you're okay.

네가 괜찮은지 보려고 잠시 들른 것뿐이야.

2 They _____ _____ _____ against him.

그들은 그에 대한 고소를 취하했다.

3 The school _____ _____ special _____ for students.

학교는 학생들을 위한 특별 프로그램을 취소했다.

4 The delivery man _____ _____ the package.

배달 기사가 택배를 가져다 놓았다.

Word Box vivid ⑱ 생생한, 선명한　charge ⑲ 기소, 고발, 비난, 책임　against 젠 ~에 맞서　delivery ⑲ 배달

A 우리말 뜻에 맞게 단어들을 연결하세요.

1 영웅으로 죽다   die   •   • the situation

2 상황을 논의하다   discuss   •   • a hero

3 ~의 꿈이 이루어지다   one's dream •   • a program

4 프로그램을 취소하다   drop   •   • comes true

B <보기>에 주어진 단어를 이용하여 우리말 뜻에 맞게 문장을 완성해 보세요. (수 일치와 시제에 주의하세요.)

> 보기   dream   drop   discuss   die

1 They fought and _____ for their freedom.
   그들은 자유를 위해 싸웠고 목숨을 잃었다.

2 We _____ the charges against him.
   우리는 그에 대한 고소를 취하했다.

3 Her _____ finally came true after hard work.
   고된 노력 끝에 그녀의 꿈이 마침내 이루어졌다.

4 They will _____ how to do the project.
   그들은 이 프로젝트를 어떻게 할지 논의할 것이다.

C 다음 문장의 빈칸에 공통으로 들어가는 단어를 써 보세요.

1 We gathered to _____ the subject.

They came to _____ the details.

2 I dreamed a vivid _____ last night.

I had a wonderful _____ about my future.

D 다음 중 옳은 표현이 쓰인 문장을 고르세요.

1 ① The sea turtle died by old age.

② The sea turtle died of old age.

2 ① We will discuss about how to solve the problem.

② We will discuss how to solve the problem.

3 ① I have dreamed of becoming a famous writer.

② I have dreamed to be a famous writer.

4 ① He just dropped at my place to see me.

② He just dropped by my place to see me.

Ⓐ Expressions 표현을 듣고, 큰 소리로 세 번씩 읽어 보세요.

MP3-041

enter

[éntər] 통 들어가다, 입력하다, 시작하다

❶ **enter a room**
방에 들어가다 ☐☐☐

❷ **enter one's password**
비밀번호를 입력하다 ☐☐☐

❸ **enter (a) college**
대학에 입학하다 ☐☐☐

❹ **enter into an agreement**
계약을[협의를] 맺다 ☐☐☐

express

[iksprés] 통 표현하다, 나타내다

❶ **express one's opinions**
견해들을 말하다 ☐☐☐

❷ **express one's feelings**
감정들을 표현하다 ☐☐☐

❸ **express interest in**
~에 관심을 보이다 ☐☐☐

❹ **express oneself**
자신을 표현하다 ☐☐☐

Ⓑ Check the Expressions

문장을 듣고, 빈칸에 알맞은 단어를 써 보세요.

MP3-042

enter

1 She _____ _____ _____ carefully.

그녀는 조심스럽게 방에 들어갔다.

★ He entered ~~into~~ a room. (X)

2 Make sure to _____ _____ _____ correctly.

당신의 비밀번호를 꼭 정확하게 입력하세요.

3 My sister was excited to _____ the _____.

우리 누나는 그 대학에 들어가서 기뻐했다.

★ enter college: 넓은 의미의 대학 진학
enter a[the] college: 어떤 구체적 대학 입학

4 The two companies _____ _____ _____ _____.

두 회사는 계약을 맺었다.

express

1 You'll be given a chance to _____ _____ _____.

너는 네 견해들을 말할 기회를 가지게 될 것이다.

2 Don't hesitate to _____ _____ _____.

너의 감정들을 표현하는 데 주저하지 말아라.

3 He _____ great _____ _____ this project.

그는 이번 프로젝트에 큰 관심을 보였다.

4 Sometimes it's hard to _____ _____.

네 자신을 표현하는 것이 때로는 힘들다.

Word Box | agreement 형 협정, 동의, 승낙   make sure 반드시 ~하다   hesitate 통 주저하다

enter / express / face / fall

MP3-043

Ⓐ Expressions 표현을 듣고, 큰 소리로 세 번씩 읽어 보세요.

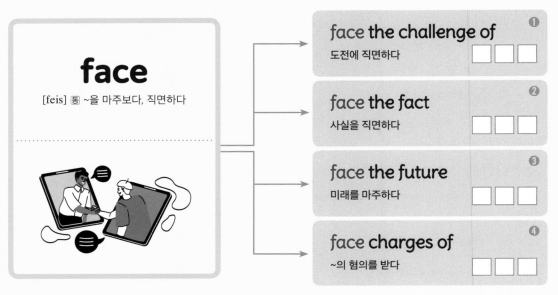

face

[feis] 통 ~을 마주보다, 직면하다

❶ **face the challenge of**
도전에 직면하다

❷ **face the fact**
사실을 직면하다

❸ **face the future**
미래를 마주하다

❹ **face charges of**
~의 혐의를 받다

fall

fell - fallen
[fɔːl] 통 떨어지다, 넘어지다, 빠지다

❶ **fall down**
떨어지다, 쓰러지다

❷ **fall in love with**
~와 사랑에 빠지다

❸ **fall asleep**
잠이 들다

❹ **fall apart**
부서지다, 무너져 내리다

Ⓑ Check the Expressions

문장을 듣고, 빈칸에 알맞은 단어를 써 보세요.

face

1 He is _____ _____ biggest _____ _____ his life.

그는 인생에서 가장 큰 도전에 직면하고 있다.

2 You have to _____ _____ _____ that you're in trouble.

너는 네가 곤경에 처했다는 사실을 받아들여야 한다. ★ I ~~was faced~~ the fact. (X)

3 Let's _____ _____ _____ and work towards our goals.

미래를 직시하고 우리의 목표를 향해 노력하자.

4 She _____ _____ _____ fraud.

그녀는 사기 혐의를 받고 있다.

fall

1 They _____ _____ from the stairs and got injured.

그들은 계단에서 떨어져서 부상을 입었다.

2 I think I _____ _____ _____ _____ you.

내 생각에 나는 너와 사랑에 빠졌던 것 같다.

3 The baby _____ _____ listening to the lullaby.

아기는 자장가를 들으며 잠이 들었다.

4 Many houses _____ _____ in the storm.

많은 집이 폭풍으로 무너졌다.

Word Box | challenge 몡 도전 fraud 몡 사기, 가짜 injured 혱 부상을 입은, 다친 lullaby 몡 자장가

A 우리말 뜻에 맞게 단어들을 연결하세요.

1 계약을 맺다   enter   •   • one's feelings

2 감정들을 표현하다   express   •   • charges of

3 혐의를 받다   face   •   • down

4 떨어지다, 쓰러지다   fall   •   • into an agreement

B <보기>에 주어진 단어를 이용하여 우리말 뜻에 맞게 문장을 완성해 보세요. (수 일치와 시제에 주의하세요.)

보기	enter fall express face

1 She _____ a room carefully.

그녀는 조심스럽게 방으로 들어갔다.

2 Sometimes it's hard to _____ yourself.

네 자신을 표현하는 것이 때로는 힘들다.

3 She _____ charges of fraud.

그녀는 사기 혐의를 받고 있다.

4 Many houses _____ apart in the storm.

많은 집이 폭풍으로 무너졌다.

1 You need to _____ your password correctly.

   I am excited to _____ a college.

2 He will _____ the challenge of his life.

   It's time to _____ the future with an open mind.

D 다음 중 옳은 표현이 쓰인 문장을 고르세요.

1 ① We entered into the classroom.

   ② We entered the classroom.

2 ① He expressed interest to this project.

   ② He expressed interest in this project.

3 ① She finally faced the fact.

   ② She finally faced to the fact.

4 ① They fell sleep listening to the music.

   ② They fell asleep listening to the music.

Expression Check List

➡ 아는 표현 앞에 √ 표시를 해 보세요. 기억나지 않는 표현은 다시 확인해 암기하세요.

√	표현	√	표현
	arrive home		call for
	arrive on time		call it a day
	arrive shortly		call someone names
	arrive late		give someone a call
	answer the question		cause damage
	answer the phone		cause a disease
	give someone an answer		cause death
	wait for an answer		cause delay
	ask a favor		change one's mind
	ask for advice		change into
	ask if		change the situation
	ask permission		change one's attitude
	it's hard to believe (that)		close one's eyes
	believe it or not		close one's mind (to)
	it is believed that		close an account
	believe in		close to death
	bring peace		control oneself
	bring chaos		lose control of
	bring it to an end		under control
	bring someone joy		remote control

√	표현	√	표현
	cook a meal		drop by
	cook something for dinner		drop the charges
	cook breakfast		drop a program
	cook something evenly		drop off
	cut along		enter a room
	cut the lawn		enter one's password
	cut one's finger		enter (a) college
	get one's hair cut		enter into an agreement
	die of		express one's opinions
	die for		express one's feelings
	would rather die		express interest in
	die a hero		express oneself
	discuss the subject		face the challenge of
	discuss the situation		face the fact
	discuss the details		face the future
	discuss how to do		face charges of
	dream of		fall down
	have a dream		fall in love with
	one's dream comes true		fall asleep
	vivid dream		fall apart

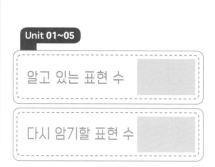

Unit 01~05

알고 있는 표현 수

다시 암기할 표현 수

Ⓐ **Expressions** 표현을 듣고, 큰 소리로 세 번씩 읽어 보세요.

MP3-045

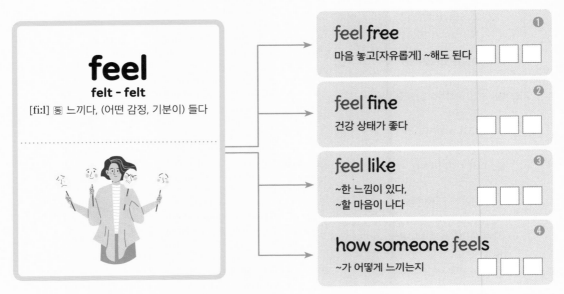

feel
felt – felt
[fi:l] 통 느끼다, (어떤 감정, 기분이) 들다

❶ feel free
마음 놓고[자유롭게] ~해도 된다 ☐☐☐

❷ feel fine
건강 상태가 좋다 ☐☐☐

❸ feel like
~한 느낌이 있다,
~할 마음이 나다 ☐☐☐

❹ how someone feels
~가 어떻게 느끼는지 ☐☐☐

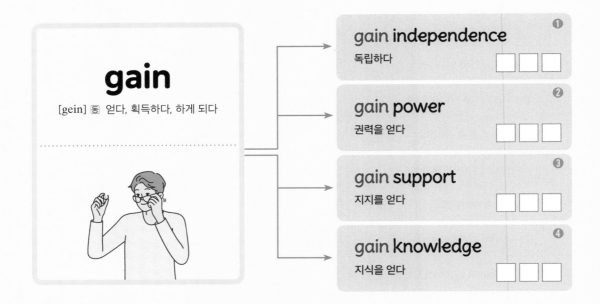

gain
[gein] 통 얻다, 획득하다, 하게 되다

❶ gain independence
독립하다 ☐☐☐

❷ gain power
권력을 얻다 ☐☐☐

❸ gain support
지지를 얻다 ☐☐☐

❹ gain knowledge
지식을 얻다 ☐☐☐

Ⓑ Check the Expressions

문장을 듣고, 빈칸에 알맞은 단어를 써 보세요.

MP3-046

feel

1 _____ _____ to ask any questions.

어떤 질문이든 자유롭게 하세요.

2 Thanks to your help, I _____ _____ now.

너의 도움 덕분에 나는 이제 몸이 좋다.

3 I _____ _____ crying after watching a movie.

영화를 보고 나는 울고 싶은 기분이었다.

4 I wonder _____ _____ _____ about it.

나는 네가 그것에 대해 어떻게 느끼는지 궁금하다.   ⭐ I'm feeling this is right. (X) I feel ~ (O)

gain

1 Korea _____ _____ on August 15, 1945.

한국은 1945년 8월 15일에 독립했다.

2 They fought for a long time to _____ _____.

그들은 권력을 얻기 위해 오랫동안 싸웠다.

3 I finally _____ _____ for my decision.

나는 마침내 내 결정에 대한 지지를 얻었다.

4 Reading books is a great way to _____ _____.

독서는 지식을 얻는 훌륭한 방법이다.

Word Box | independence 명 독립   support 명 지지 동 지지하다, 지원하다   thanks to ~의 덕분에

feel / gain / help / hold

Ⓐ Expressions 표현을 듣고, 큰 소리로 세 번씩 읽어 보세요.

MP3-047

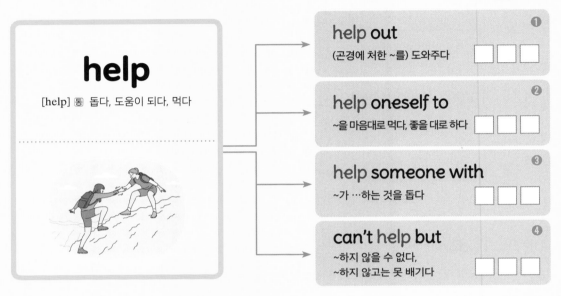

help

[help] 통 돕다, 도움이 되다, 먹다

help out ①
(곤경에 처한 ~를) 도와주다 ☐ ☐ ☐

help oneself to ②
~을 마음대로 먹다, 좋을 대로 하다 ☐ ☐ ☐

help someone with ③
~가 …하는 것을 돕다 ☐ ☐ ☐

can't help but ④
~하지 않을 수 없다,
~하지 않고는 못 배기다 ☐ ☐ ☐

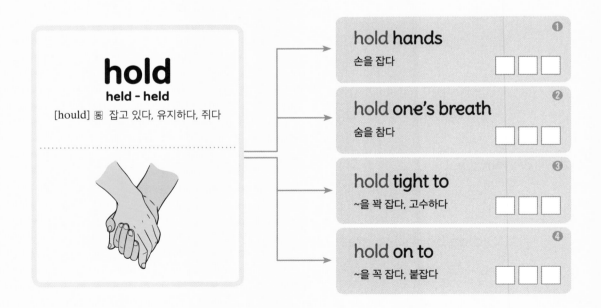

hold
held - held
[hould] 통 잡고 있다, 유지하다, 쥐다

hold hands ①
손을 잡다 ☐ ☐ ☐

hold one's breath ②
숨을 참다 ☐ ☐ ☐

hold tight to ③
~을 꽉 잡다, 고수하다 ☐ ☐ ☐

hold on to ④
~을 꼭 잡다, 붙잡다 ☐ ☐ ☐

Ⓑ Check the Expressions

문장을 듣고, 빈칸에 알맞은 단어를 써 보세요.

MP3-048

help

1 I'll volunteer to _____ _____ at the animal shelter.

나는 동물 보호소 일을 돕기 위해 자원봉사 할 것이다.

2 _____ _____ _____ the snacks on the table.

탁자에 있는 간식을 편하게 드세요.

3 Could you _____ _____ _____ moving this box, please?

내가 이 상자 옮기는 것 좀 도와주시겠어요?

4 I _____ _____ _____ wonder what will happen next.

나는 다음에 무슨 일이 일어날지 궁금해서 못 참겠다.

hold

1 She burst into tears while _____ my _____.

그녀는 내 손을 잡고 울음을 터뜨렸다.

2 _____ _____ _____ and count to ten.

너는 숨을 참고 10까지 세어라.

3 I'll _____ _____ _____ my beliefs and values.

나는 나의 신념과 가치를 고수할 것이다.

4 Don't forget to _____ _____ _____ the handlebars.

손잡이 꼭 잡는 것을 잊지 마세요.

Word Box | shelter 명 보호소, 대피, 주거지   value 명 가치 통 소중하게 생각하다   handlebar 명 손잡이

A 우리말 뜻에 맞게 단어들을 연결하세요.

1 자유롭게 ~해도 된다   feel •   • free

2 지식을 얻다   gain •   • oneself to

3 ~을 마음대로 먹다   help •   • knowledge

4 손을 잡다   hold •   • hands

B <보기>에 주어진 단어를 이용하여 우리말 뜻에 맞게 문장을 완성해 보세요. (수 일치와 시제에 주의하세요.)

보기	help feel hold gain

1 I _____ like crying after watching a movie.
   영화를 보고 나는 울고 싶은 기분이었다.

2 I finally _____ support for my decision.
   나는 마침내 내 결정에 대한 지지를 얻었다.

3 I can't _____ but wonder what will happen next.
   나는 다음에 무슨 일이 일어날지 궁금해서 못 참겠다.

4 _____ your breath and count to ten.
   너는 숨을 참고 10까지 세어라.

C 다음 문장의 빈칸에 공통으로 들어가는 단어를 써 보세요.

1 They fought to _____ power.

We wanted to _____ support from teachers.

☐

2 I'll volunteer to _____ out at the school event.

Could you _____ me with my homework?

☐

D 다음 중 옳은 표현이 쓰인 문장을 고르세요.

1 ① I feel fine now after taking a rest.

② I feeling fine now after taking a rest.

2 ① They gained an independence 100 years ago.

② They gained independence 100 years ago.

3 ① I can't help but wonder why he said that.

② I can't help but to wondering why he said that.

4 ① I'll hold tight to my dreams and never give up.

② I'll hold tightly my dreams and never give up.

hope / know / laugh / let

Ⓐ Expressions 표현을 듣고, 큰 소리로 세 번씩 읽어 보세요.

MP3-049

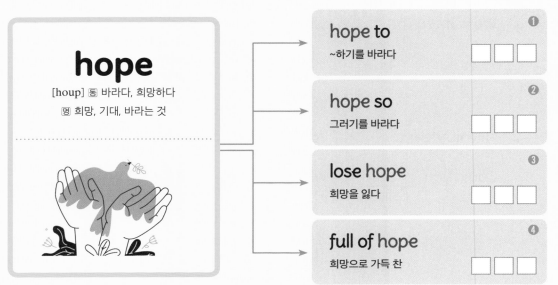

hope

[houp] 동 바라다, 희망하다
명 희망, 기대, 바라는 것

❶ **hope to**
~하기를 바라다

❷ **hope so**
그러기를 바라다

❸ **lose hope**
희망을 잃다

❹ **full of hope**
희망으로 가득 찬

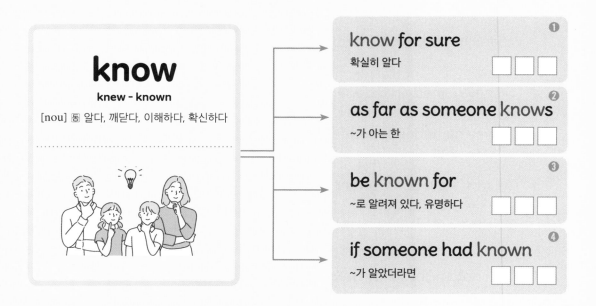

know

knew - known

[nou] 동 알다, 깨닫다, 이해하다, 확신하다

❶ **know for sure**
확실히 알다

❷ **as far as someone knows**
~가 아는 한

❸ **be known for**
~로 알려져 있다, 유명하다

❹ **if someone had known**
~가 알았더라면

Ⓑ Check the Expressions

문장을 듣고, 빈칸에 알맞은 단어를 써 보세요.

hope

1 We're _____ _____ get tickets to the concert.

우리는 콘서트 입장권 구하기를 희망하고 있다.

2 They said he would be back, and I _____ _____.

그들은 그가 돌아올 것이라고 말했고, 나도 그러기를 바란다.

3 It's important not to _____ _____.

희망을 잃지 않는 것이 중요하다.

4 She started her new journey _____ _____ _____.

그녀는 희망에 가득차서 새로운 여행을 시작했다.

know

1 You'll _____ _____ _____ after the test results come out.

검사 결과가 나와야 당신이 확실히 알 수 있을 것이다.

2 _____ _____ _____ _____ _____, she didn't lie to us.

내가 아는 한 그녀는 우리에게 거짓말하지 않았다.

3 Egypt _____ _____ _____ its ancient pyramids.

이집트는 고대 피라미드들로 유명하다.

4 _____ _____ _____ _____ it was going to rain, I would have left earlier.

비가 올 줄 알았더라면, 나는 더 일찍 떠났을 텐데.

⭐ I'm knowing it. (X) I know ~ (O)

Word Box | journey 몡 여행 동 여행하다 result 몡 결과 ancient 혱 고대의, 아주 오래된

Ⓐ **Expressions** 표현을 듣고, 큰 소리로 세 번씩 읽어 보세요.

MP3-051

laugh

[læf] 통 (소리내어) 웃다

Ha-ha

❶ **laugh at**
~에 대해 웃다,
~를 비웃다[놀리다]

❷ **make someone laugh**
~를 웃게 하다

❸ **begin to laugh**
웃기 시작하다

❹ **try not to laugh**
웃지 않으려 노력하다

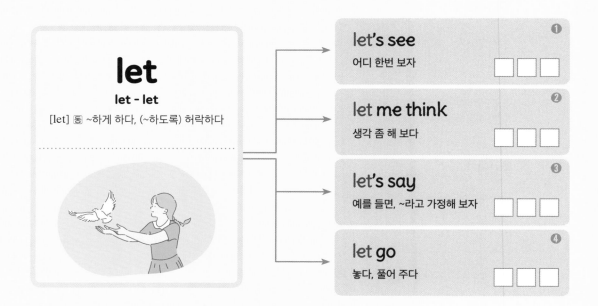

let

let - let

[let] 통 ~하게 하다, (~하도록) 허락하다

❶ **let's see**
어디 한번 보자

❷ **let me think**
생각 좀 해 보다

❸ **let's say**
예를 들면, ~라고 가정해 보자

❹ **let go**
놓다, 풀어 주다

Ⓑ Check the Expressions

문장을 듣고, 빈칸에 알맞은 단어를 써 보세요.

laugh

1 It's not polite to _____ _____ someone.

누군가를 비웃는 것은 무례한 일이다.

2 He always _____ _____ _____.

그는 항상 나를 웃게 한다.

3 They _____ _____ _____ at his joke.

그들은 그의 농담에 웃기 시작했다.

4 I _____ _____ _____ _____ at his silly mistake.

나는 그의 우스꽝스러운 실수에 웃지 않으려 노력했다.

let

1 _____ _____ if we can find a solution to this problem.

우리가 이 문제에 대한 해결책을 찾을 수 있을지 한번 보자.

2 _____ _____ _____ for a moment before I respond.

답변하기 전에 잠시 생각 좀 해 볼게요.   ★ Let me ~~thinking~~. (X) Let me ~~to~~ think. (X)

3 I can give you a discount, _____ _____, 50%.

제가 할인해 드릴 수 있어요, 예를 들면 50% 정도요.

4 She decided to _____ _____ of her worries.

그녀는 걱정을 떨쳐 버리기로 결심했다.

Word Box silly 혱 바보 같은, 우스꽝스러운, 철없는 discount 몡 할인 worry 몡 걱정거리, 걱정되는 일 뫙 걱정하다

A 우리말 뜻에 맞게 단어들을 연결하세요.

1 희망으로 가득 찬   full of   •   • for sure

2 확실히 알다   know   •   • at

3 비웃다   laugh   •   • say

4 예를 들어   let's   •   • hope

B <보기>에 주어진 단어를 이용하여 우리말 뜻에 맞게 문장을 완성해 보세요. (수 일치와 시제에 주의하세요.)

보기	hope know laugh let

1 I'm _____ to get tickets to the concert.
나는 콘서트 입장권 구하기를 희망하고 있다.

2 If I had _____ it was going to rain, I would have left earlier.
비가 올 줄 알았더라면, 나는 더 일찍 떠났을 텐데.

3 I tried not to _____ at his mistake.
나는 그의 실수에 웃지 않으려 노력했다.

4 _____ me think for a moment before I respond.
답변하기 전에 잠시 생각 좀 해 볼게요.

C 다음 문장의 빈칸에 공통으로 들어가는 단어를 써 보세요.

1 They said he would be back, and I _____ so.

It's important not to lose _____.

[   ]

2 It's not polite to _____ at someone.

She began to _____ at my joke.

[   ]

D 다음 중 옳은 표현이 쓰인 문장을 고르세요.

1 ① I'm hoping to travel to the Europe.

② I'm hoping travel to the Europe.

2 ① Paris is known to its beautiful architecture.

② Paris is known for its beautiful architecture.

3 ① She always makes me laughing.

② She always makes me laugh.

4 ① It's time to let go of the past.

② It's time to let to go of the past.

lie / like / look / matter

MP3-053

Ⓐ **Expressions** 표현을 듣고, 큰 소리로 세 번씩 읽어 보세요.

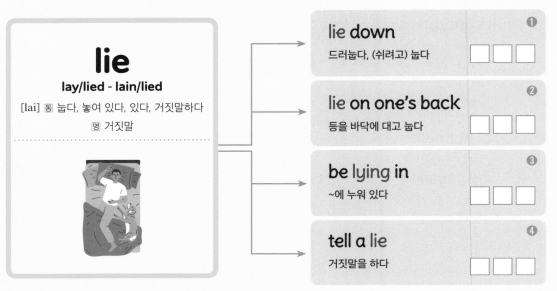

lie

lay/lied - lain/lied

[lai] 동 눕다, 놓여 있다, 있다, 거짓말하다
명 거짓말

❶ **lie down**
드러눕다, (쉬려고) 눕다

❷ **lie on one's back**
등을 바닥에 대고 눕다

❸ **be lying in**
~에 누워 있다

❹ **tell a lie**
거짓말을 하다

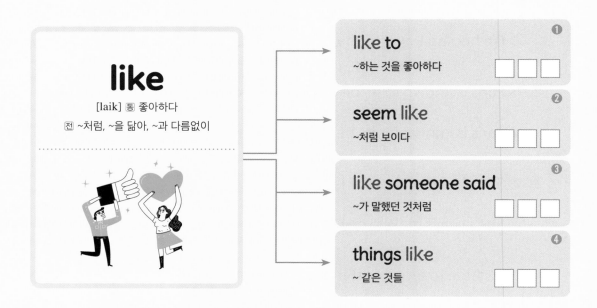

like

[laik] 동 좋아하다
전 ~처럼, ~을 닮아, ~과 다름없이

❶ **like to**
~하는 것을 좋아하다

❷ **seem like**
~처럼 보이다

❸ **like someone said**
~가 말했던 것처럼

❹ **things like**
~ 같은 것들

Ⓑ Check the Expressions

문장을 듣고, 빈칸에 알맞은 단어를 써 보세요.

MP3-054

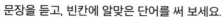
lie

1 It's nice to _____ _____ on the grass and rest.

잔디밭에 누워 쉬는 것이 좋다.

2 _____ _____ _____ _____ and relax your muscles.

등을 바닥에 대고 누워 근육의 긴장을 푸세요.

3 The puppy _____ _____ _____ the sun, sleeping.

강아지가 햇빛에 누워서 잠을 자고 있다.

4 He promised he would never _____ _____ _____.

그는 절대 거짓말을 하지 않겠다고 약속했다.

like

1 She _____ _____ read before bedtime.

그녀는 잠들기 전에 책 읽는 것을 좋아한다.

⭐ I am liking dogs. (X) I like ~ (O)

2 It _____ _____ a good idea to me.

나에게는 그게 좋은 생각인 것처럼 보인다.

3 _____ _____ _____ before, you need to finish it by 6 o'clock.

내가 전에 말했듯이 너는 그것을 6시까지 마쳐야 한다.

4 I like sweet _____ _____ candies and caramels.

나는 사탕이나 캐러멜 같은 단것들을 좋아한다.

Word Box | lie (눕다) - lay (누웠다) - lain   lie (거짓말하다) - lied (거짓말했다) - lied

Ⓐ **Expressions** 표현을 듣고, 큰 소리로 세 번씩 읽어 보세요.

MP3-055

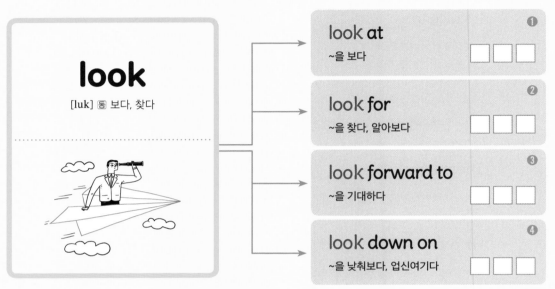

look

[luk] 동 보다, 찾다

❶ **look at**
~을 보다

❷ **look for**
~을 찾다, 알아보다

❸ **look forward to**
~을 기대하다

❹ **look down on**
~을 낮춰보다, 업신여기다

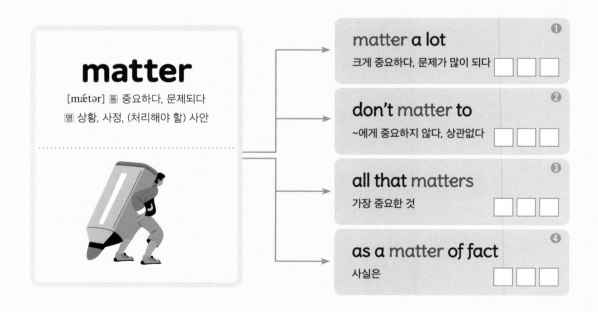

matter

[mǽtər] 동 중요하다, 문제되다
명 상황, 사정, (처리해야 할) 사안

❶ **matter a lot**
크게 중요하다, 문제가 많이 되다

❷ **don't matter to**
~에게 중요하지 않다, 상관없다

❸ **all that matters**
가장 중요한 것

❹ **as a matter of fact**
사실은

Ⓑ Check the Expressions

문장을 듣고, 빈칸에 알맞은 단어를 써 보세요.

MP3-056

look

1 The little prince was _____ _____ the sunset.

어린 왕자는 석양을 바라보고 있었다.

★ I'm looking ~~to~~ the puppy. (X)

2 I'm _____ _____ a private tutor.

나는 개인 과외 교사를 알아보고 있다.

3 We _____ _____ _____ seeing you soon.

우리는 너를 곧 만나기를 기대한다.

4 He always _____ _____ _____ others.

그는 항상 다른 사람들을 얕잡아 본다.

matter

1 Our teacher's opinion _____ _____ _____ to us.

우리 선생님의 의견은 우리에게 매우 중요하다.

2 Whether he likes it or not, it _____ _____ _____ me.

그가 그것을 좋아하든 말든, 나에게는 중요하지 않다.

3 _____ _____ _____ is that we're together.

가장 중요한 것은 우리가 함께 있다는 것이다.

4 _____ _____ _____ _____ _____ , I didn't like it.

사실 나는 그것을 좋아하지 않았다.

Word Box | private 형 개인 소유의, 사적인 tutor 명 개인 지도 교사 whether 접 ~인지 아닌지

A 우리말 뜻에 맞게 단어들을 연결하세요.

1 드러눕다   lie   •   • a lot

2 ~가 말했던 것처럼   like   •   • down

3 ~을 기대하다   look   •   • someone said

4 크게 중요하다   matter   •   • forward to

B <보기>에 주어진 단어를 이용하여 우리말 뜻에 맞게 문장을 완성해 보세요. (수 일치와 시제에 주의하세요.)

보기	look lie matter like

1 The kitten is _____ in the sun, sleeping.

새끼 고양이가 햇빛에 누워 잠을 자고 있다.

2 She _____ to read before bedtime.

그녀는 잠들기 전에 책 읽는 것을 좋아한다.

3 He is _____ for a new job opportunity.

그는 새로운 일자리 기회를 알아보고 있다.

4 As a _____ of fact, I didn't like it.

사실 나는 그것을 좋아하지 않았다.

C 다음 문장의 빈칸에 공통으로 들어가는 단어를 써 보세요.

1 _____ I said before, you should be polite to our guests.

She likes sweet things _____ candies and caramels.

```

```

2 Whether he likes it or not, it doesn't _____ to me.

The opinions of my family _____ a lot to us.

```

```

D 다음 문장에서 틀린 부분을 찾아 바르게 고쳐 써 보세요.

1 It's nice to lay down on the grass and rest.

→ _____

2 It seem to like a good idea to me.

→ _____

3 The little prince was looking to the sunset.

→ _____

4 All that matter is that we're together.

→ _____

open / pass / pay / play

Ⓐ **Expressions** 표현을 듣고, 큰 소리로 세 번씩 읽어 보세요.

MP3-057

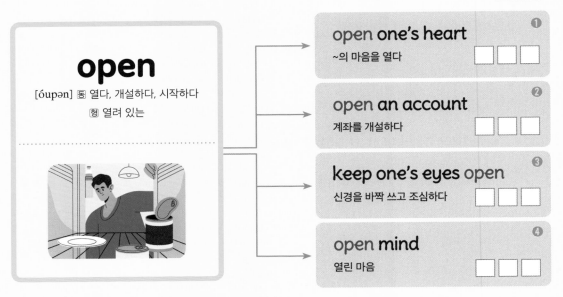

open

[óupən] 통 열다, 개설하다, 시작하다
형 열려 있는

❶ open one's heart
~의 마음을 열다 ☐ ☐ ☐

❷ open an account
계좌를 개설하다 ☐ ☐ ☐

❸ keep one's eyes open
신경을 바짝 쓰고 조심하다 ☐ ☐ ☐

❹ open mind
열린 마음 ☐ ☐ ☐

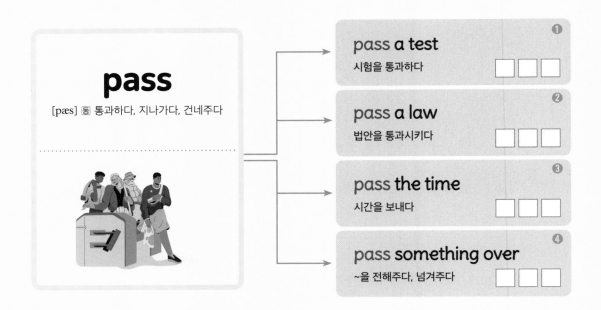

pass

[pæs] 통 통과하다, 지나가다, 건네주다

❶ pass a test
시험을 통과하다 ☐ ☐ ☐

❷ pass a law
법안을 통과시키다 ☐ ☐ ☐

❸ pass the time
시간을 보내다 ☐ ☐ ☐

❹ pass something over
~을 전해주다, 넘겨주다 ☐ ☐ ☐

Ⓑ Check the Expressions

문장을 듣고, 빈칸에 알맞은 단어를 써 보세요.

open

1 Don't be afraid to _____ _____ _____ to new friends.

새로운 친구들에게 당신 마음을 여는 것을 두려워하지 마세요.

2 More people are _____ online _____.

더 많은 사람이 온라인 계좌들을 개설하고 있다. ⭐ open an account online, open an online account (O)

3 _____ _____ _____ _____ for important details.

중요한 세부 사항에 주의를 기울이세요.

4 Listen to different opinions with an _____ _____.

열린 마음으로 다른 의견들을 들어 보세요.

pass

1 I was happy to _____ _____ _____.

나는 시험에 통과해서 기뻤다.

2 The city council voted to _____ _____ _____.

시의회는 법안을 통과시키기 위해 투표했다.

3 We played games to _____ _____ _____.

우리는 시간을 보내기 위해 게임을 했다.

4 If you finish reading a book, you can _____ _____ _____ to her.

책을 다 읽으면 그것을 그녀에게 전해주면 돼.

> **Word Box** | council 몡 의회, 위원회   vote 툉 투표하다

open / pass / pay / play

Ⓐ **Expressions** 표현을 듣고, 큰 소리로 세 번씩 읽어 보세요.

MP3-059

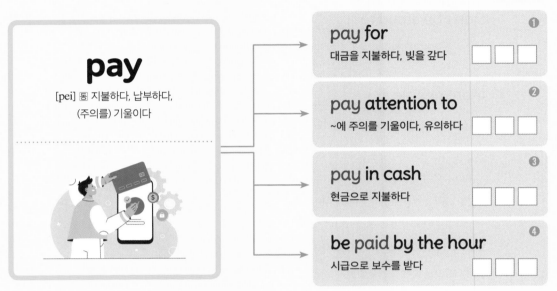

pay

[pei] 통 지불하다, 납부하다, (주의를) 기울이다

❶ pay for
대금을 지불하다, 빚을 갚다 ☐☐☐

❷ pay attention to
~에 주의를 기울이다, 유의하다 ☐☐☐

❸ pay in cash
현금으로 지불하다 ☐☐☐

❹ be paid by the hour
시급으로 보수를 받다 ☐☐☐

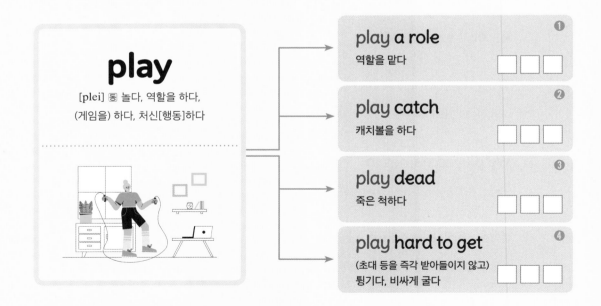

play

[plei] 통 놀다, 역할을 하다, (게임을) 하다, 처신[행동]하다

❶ play a role
역할을 맡다 ☐☐☐

❷ play catch
캐치볼을 하다 ☐☐☐

❸ play dead
죽은 척하다 ☐☐☐

❹ play hard to get
(초대 등을 즉각 받아들이지 않고) 튕기다, 비싸게 굴다 ☐☐☐

Ⓑ Check the Expressions

문장을 듣고, 빈칸에 알맞은 단어를 써 보세요.

pay

1 My parents _____ _____ my swimming lessons.

부모님이 내 수영 강습비를 내셨다. ★ She will pay the tickets. (X)

2 Please _____ _____ _____ the road while driving.

운전 중엔 도로 상황에 주의를 기울이세요.

3 Would you prefer to _____ _____ _____?

현금으로 결제하시는 편이 좋으신가요?

4 The employees _____ _____ _____ _____ _____.

그 직원들은 시급으로 보수를 받는다.

play

1 Technology _____ _____ important _____ in our future.

기술은 우리의 미래에 중요한 역할을 한다.

2 I used to _____ _____ with my friends.

나는 친구들과 캐치볼을 하곤 했다.

3 He thought it was safer to _____ _____.

그는 죽은 척하는 것이 더 안전하다고 생각했다.

4 Jenny is _____ _____ _____ _____ with the invitation.

제니는 초대에 갈지 말지 튕기고 있다.

> **Word Box** | catch 명 캐치볼 놀이   prefer 동 ~을 더 좋아하다, 선택하다

A 우리말 뜻에 맞게 단어들을 연결하세요.

1	마음을 열다	open •	•	a test
2	시험을 통과하다	pass •	•	dead
3	시급으로 보수를 받다	be paid •	•	one's heart
4	죽은 척하다	play •	•	by the hour

B <보기>에 주어진 단어를 이용하여 우리말 뜻에 맞게 문장을 완성해 보세요. (수 일치와 시제에 주의하세요.)

보기
pass   open   play   pay

1 People are _____ online accounts to play games.

사람들은 게임을 하기 위해 온라인 계좌를 개설하고 있다.

2 They are working to _____ a law.

그들은 법안을 통과시키기 위해 일하고 있다.

3 She _____ for her vacation package.

그녀는 자신의 휴가 패키지 비용을 지불했다.

4 Education _____ an important role in our future.

교육은 우리의 미래에 중요한 역할을 한다.

C 다음 문장의 빈칸에 공통으로 들어가는 단어를 써 보세요.

1 Don't be afraid to _____ your heart to new experiences.

I'm going to _____ an online account.

```
┌─────────────────────┐
│                     │
│                     │
└─────────────────────┘
```

2 Please _____ attention to your health.

Are you going to _____ in cash or by a credit card?

```
┌─────────────────────┐
│                     │
│                     │
└─────────────────────┘
```

D 다음 문장에서 틀린 부분을 찾아 바르게 고쳐 써 보세요.

1 Keep your eye open for important details.

→ _____

2 If you finish reading a book, you can pass over to her.

→ _____

3 Please pay attention the road while driving.

→ _____

4 I used to play a catch with my friends.

→ _____

Ⓐ **Expressions** 표현을 듣고, 큰 소리로 세 번씩 읽어 보세요.

MP3-061

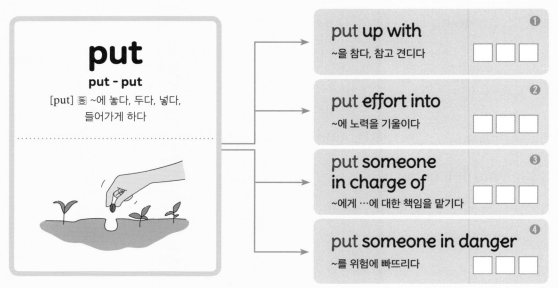

put

put - put

[put] 통 ~에 놓다, 두다, 넣다, 들어가게 하다

put up with ❶
~을 참다, 참고 견디다
□□□

put effort into ❷
~에 노력을 기울이다
□□□

put someone in charge of ❸
~에게 …에 대한 책임을 맡기다
□□□

put someone in danger ❹
~를 위험에 빠뜨리다
□□□

raise

[reiz] 통 들어올리다, 높이다, 모으다

raise one's hand ❶
손을 들다
□□□

raise one's voice ❷
목소리를[언성을] 높이다
□□□

raise money ❸
돈을 마련하다
□□□

raise the alarm ❹
경보를 울리다, 경고를 하다
□□□

Ⓑ Check the Expressions

문장을 듣고, 빈칸에 알맞은 단어를 써 보세요.

put

1 I can't _____ _____ _____ his rude behavior.

나는 그의 무례한 행동을 참을 수가 없다.

2 You'll need to _____ _____ _____ learning English.

너는 영어를 배우는 데 노력해야 할 것이다.   ⭐ I ~~do~~ effort into learning English. (X)

3 The coach _____ _____ _____ _____ _____ leading the exercise.

코치님은 나에게 훈련 책임을 맡기셨다.

4 It can _____ _____ _____ _____ of serious accidents.

그것은 당신을 심각한 사고의 위험에 빠뜨릴 수 있다.

raise

1 _____ _____ _____ if you have a question.

질문이 있으면 손을 드세요.

2 It's important to _____ _____ _____ and show your confidence.

네 목소리를 높여서 자신감을 보여 주는 것이 중요하다.

3 The singers _____ _____ for charity.

가수들은 자선 모금을 하였다.

4 He knocked on doors to _____ _____ _____.

그는 경고를 하기 위해 문을 두드렸다.

Word Box | behavior 명 행동   confidence 명 확신, 자신감   charity 명 자선, 너그러움

put / raise / reach / read

Ⓐ **Expressions** 표현을 듣고, 큰 소리로 세 번씩 읽어 보세요.

MP3-063

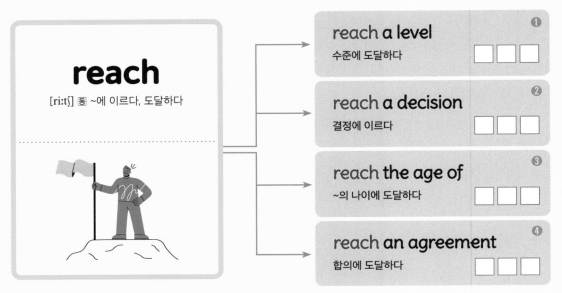

reach

[riːtʃ] 동 ~에 이르다, 도달하다

❶ reach **a level**
수준에 도달하다

❷ reach **a decision**
결정에 이르다

❸ reach **the age of**
~의 나이에 도달하다

❹ reach **an agreement**
합의에 도달하다

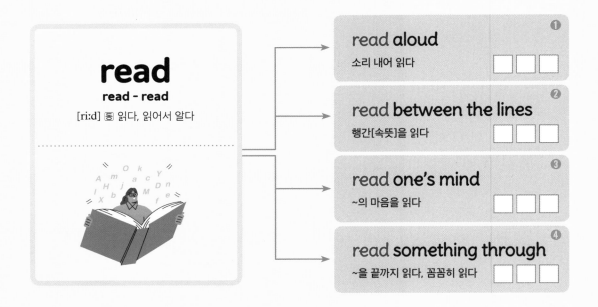

read
read - read

[riːd] 동 읽다, 읽어서 알다

❶ read **aloud**
소리 내어 읽다

❷ read **between the lines**
행간[속뜻]을 읽다

❸ read **one's mind**
~의 마음을 읽다

❹ read **something through**
~을 끝까지 읽다, 꼼꼼히 읽다

Ⓑ Check the Expressions

문장을 듣고, 빈칸에 알맞은 단어를 써 보세요.

MP3-064

---

reach

1 They _____ _____ high _____ of academic achievement.

그들은 학술적 성취 면에서 높은 수준에 도달했다.

2 The judge finally _____ _____ _____.

판사는 마침내 결정을 내렸다.

3 She will _____ _____ _____ _____ 18 next month.

그녀는 다음 달이면 18살이 된다.

4 It took several hours to _____ _____ _____.

합의에 이르기까지 여러 시간이 걸렸다.

> ⭐ They finally reached ~~to~~ home. (X)
> They finally reached ~~to~~ the school. (X)

---

read

1 When I can't concentrate, I _____ _____.

나는 집중이 되지 않을 때 큰소리로 읽는다.

2 He _____ _____ _____ _____ in her messages.

그는 그녀의 메시지에서 속뜻을 읽었다.

3 My teacher seems to _____ _____ _____.

우리 선생님은 내 마음을 읽으시는 것 같다.

4 I'm sorry that I haven't _____ _____ _____ yet.

미안하지만 나는 아직 그것을 끝까지 읽지 못했어요.

Word Box | academic 혱 학업의, 학교의, 학문의   concentrate 동 집중하다, 집중시키다

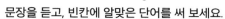

A 우리말 뜻에 맞게 단어들을 연결하세요.

1 참다   put •   • one's voice

2 ~의 목소리를 높이다   raise •   • the age of

3 ~의 나이에 도달하다   reach •   • one's mind

4 ~의 마음을 읽다   read •   • up with

B <보기>에 주어진 단어를 이용하여 우리말 뜻에 맞게 문장을 완성해 보세요. (수 일치와 시제에 주의하세요.)

> 보기
>
> put   read   raise   reach

1 Playing with fire can _____ you in danger.

불장난을 하는 것은 너를 위험에 빠뜨릴 수 있다.

2 The students _____ money for the school events.

학생들은 학교 행사를 위해 모금 활동을 했다.

3 She _____ a high level of success in her career.

그녀는 자신의 일에서 높은 성취를 이루었다.

4 I always _____ aloud when I practice my presentation.

나는 프레젠테이션을 연습할 때 항상 큰소리로 읽는다.

C 다음 문장의 빈칸에 공통으로 들어가는 단어를 써 보세요.

1 I hope we can _____ a decision by tomorrow.

It took several days to _____ an agreement.

> [   ]

2 My mother seems to _____ my mind.

I'm sorry that I haven't _____ it through yet.

> [   ]

D 다음 문장에서 틀린 부분을 찾아 바르게 고쳐 써 보세요.

1 You'll need to put effort to learning English.

→ _____

2 Raise hand if you have a question.

→ _____

3 The judge finally reached decision.

→ _____

4 He read between the line in her messages.

→ _____

Expression Check List

→ 아는 표현 앞에 √ 표시를 해 보세요. 기억나지 않는 표현은 다시 확인해 암기하세요.

√	표현	√	표현
	feel free		know for sure
	feel fine		as far as someone knows
	feel like		be known for
	how someone feels		if someone had known
	gain independence		laugh at
	gain power		make someone laugh
	gain support		begin to laugh
	gain knowledge		try not to laugh
	help out		let's see
	help oneself to		let me think
	help someone with		let's say
	can't help but		let go
	hold hands		lie down
	hold one's breath		lie on one's back
	hold tight to		be lying in
	hold on to		tell a lie
	hope to		like to
	hope so		seem like
	lose hope		like someone said
	full of hope		things like

√	표현	√	표현
	look at		play a role
	look for		play catch
	look forward to		play dead
	look down on		play hard to get
	matter a lot		put up with
	don't matter to		put effort into
	all that matters		put someone in charge of
	as a matter of fact		put someone in danger
	open one's heart		raise one's hand
	open an account		raise one's voice
	keep one's eyes open		raise money
	open mind		raise the alarm
	pass a test		reach a level
	pass a law		reach a decision
	pass the time		reach the age of
	pass something over		reach an agreement
	pay for		read aloud
	pay attention to		read between the lines
	pay in cash		read one's mind
	be paid by the hour		read something through

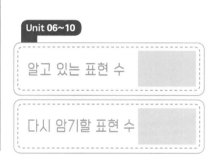

Unit 06~10

알고 있는 표현 수

다시 암기할 표현 수

receive / remember / respect / return

Ⓐ Expressions 표현을 듣고, 큰 소리로 세 번씩 읽어 보세요.

MP3-065

receive
[risíːv] 통 받다, 받아들이다, (부상 등을) 입다

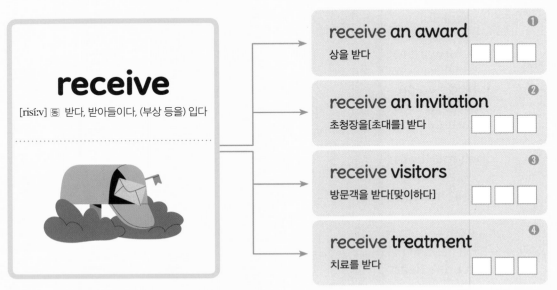

❶ **receive an award**
상을 받다 ☐☐☐

❷ **receive an invitation**
초청장을[초대를] 받다 ☐☐☐

❸ **receive visitors**
방문객을 받다[맞이하다] ☐☐☐

❹ **receive treatment**
치료를 받다 ☐☐☐

remember
[rimémbər] 통 기억하다, 기억나다, 명심하다

❶ **remember well**
잘 기억하다 ☐☐☐

❷ **remember to**
~할 것을 기억하다 ☐☐☐

❸ **hardly remember**
거의 기억하지 못하다 ☐☐☐

❹ **as far as someone remembers**
~가 기억하는 한 ☐☐☐

ⒷCheck the Expressions

문장을 듣고, 빈칸에 알맞은 단어를 써 보세요.

---

receive

1 She _____ _____ _____ from the mayor.

그녀는 시장님께 상을 받았다.

2 I _____ _____ _____ from the board.

나는 위원회로부터 초청장을 받았다.

3 My grandmother loves to _____ _____.

우리 할머니는 손님 맞이하는 것을 좋아하신다.

4 They _____ _____ in the hospital.

그들은 병원에서 치료를 받았다.

remember

1 I _____ _____ my first day at school.

나는 학교에서의 첫날을 잘 기억한다.

2 _____ _____ review your notes before the exam.

시험 전에 필기한 것을 복습하는 것을 기억하세요.

3 I _____ _____ what the teacher said in the class.

나는 선생님께서 수업 때 하신 말씀이 거의 기억나지 않는다.

4 _____ _____ _____ _____ _____, he was a good man.

내가 기억하는 한, 그는 좋은 사람이었다. ⭐ I am remembering her. (X) I remember ~ (O)

> **Word Box** | award 명 상 treatment 명 치료, 처치, 대우 mayor 명 시장

Unit 11 receive / remember / respect / return

Ⓐ Expressions 표현을 듣고, 큰 소리로 세 번씩 읽어 보세요.

MP3-067

respect

[rispékt] 图 존경하다, 존중하다
图 존경(심), 존중, 경의

❶ respect for
~에 대한 존중,
~ 때문에 존경하다 ☐☐☐

❷ respect one's privacy
~의 사생활을 존중하다 ☐☐☐

❸ respect human rights
인권을 존중하다 ☐☐☐

❹ deserve respect
존경받을 만하다 ☐☐☐

return

[ritə́:rn] 图 돌아오다, 돌아가다,
돌려주다, 반납하다

❶ return to
~로 돌아가다 ☐☐☐

❷ return from
~에서 돌아오다 ☐☐☐

❸ return one's call
응답 전화를 해주다 ☐☐☐

❹ return the favor
은혜를 갚다, 보답하다 ☐☐☐

ⒷCheck the Expressions

문장을 듣고, 빈칸에 알맞은 단어를 써 보세요.

MP3-068

respect

1 We should show _____ _____ our elders.

우리는 연세 드신 분들에 대한 존경심을 보여야 한다.

2 I _____ _____ _____ and won't ask further questions.

나는 당신의 사생활을 존중하고 추가 질문을 하지 않을 것이다.

3 We were taught to _____ _____ _____.

우리는 인권을 존중하라고 배웠다.

4 He _____ _____ due to his loyalty.

그는 충성심 때문에 존경받을 만하다.

return

1 The cleaning robot _____ _____ a charging station.

청소 로봇은 충전소로 돌아갔다.

⭐ He returned ~~to~~ home. (X)

2 He _____ _____ his long adventure.

그는 긴 모험에서 돌아왔다.

3 I asked her to _____ _____ _____.

나는 그녀에게 내 전화에 답해 달라고 부탁했다.

4 I hope I can _____ _____ _____ someday.

나는 언젠가 보답을 할 수 있기를 바란다.

Word Box | deserve 통 ~을 받을 만하다, 누릴 자격이 있다 elders 명 어른들, 원로들, 연장자 loyalty 명 충성, 충성심

A 우리말 뜻에 맞게 단어들을 연결하세요.

1 상을 받다   receive •   • someone remembers

2 ~가 기억하는 한   as far as •   • one's privacy

3 사생활을 존중하다   respect •   • an award

4 보답하다   return   •   • the favor

B <보기>에 주어진 단어를 이용하여 우리말 뜻에 맞게 문장을 완성해 보세요. (수 일치와 시제에 주의하세요.)

보기	remember receive return respect

1 He _____ treatment for his injuries.
그는 상처를 치료 받았다.

2 _____ to turn off the lights when you go out.
외출할 때 불 끄는 것을 기억하세요.

3 She deserves _____ for her leadership.
그녀는 리더십 때문에 존경받을 만하다.

4 My father _____ from his business trip.
우리 아빠는 출장에서 돌아오셨다.

C 다음 문장의 빈칸에 공통으로 들어가는 단어를 써 보세요.

1 I always _____ to review the directions before the task.

I hardly _____ the passwords to my online accounts.

2 We should show _____ for different cultures.

It is important to _____ human rights.

D 다음 문장에서 틀린 부분을 찾아 바르게 고쳐 써 보세요.

1 I received invitation from the board.

→ _____

2 I am remembering well my first day at school.

→ _____

3 He deserves to respect due to his loyalty.

→ _____

4 The cleaning robot returned a charging station.

→ _____

Ⓐ Expressions 표현을 듣고, 큰 소리로 세 번씩 읽어 보세요.

MP3-069

run
ran - run
[rʌn] 통 달리다, 달아나다, 실시하다,
~에 전해지다

❶ **run away**
도망치다

❷ **run for one's life**
필사적으로 달리다[도망치다]

❸ **run some tests**
테스트[검사]를 해보다

❹ **run in one's family**
~의 집안 내력이다, 유전하다

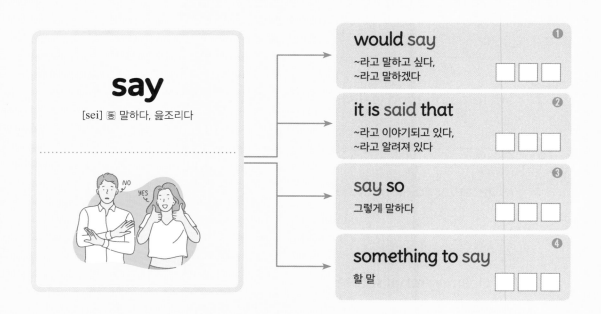

say
[sei] 통 말하다, 읊조리다

❶ **would say**
~라고 말하고 싶다,
~라고 말하겠다

❷ **it is said that**
~라고 이야기되고 있다,
~라고 알려져 있다

❸ **say so**
그렇게 말하다

❹ **something to say**
할 말

ⓑ Check the Expressions

문장을 듣고, 빈칸에 알맞은 단어를 써 보세요.

run

1 The prisoner _____ _____ from the prison.

죄수는 감옥에서 도망쳤다.

2 They had to _____ _____ _____ _____ to find shelter.

그들은 피신처를 찾기 위해 필사적으로 달려야 했다.

3 Scientists will _____ _____ _____ to check for errors.

과학자들은 오류를 확인하기 위해 몇 가지 테스트를 할 것이다.

4 Musical talent seems to _____ _____ _____ _____.

음악적 재능은 우리 집안 내력인 것 같다.

say

1 I _____ _____ reading is the most exciting adventure.

나는 독서가 가장 신나는 모험이라고 말하고 싶다.

2 _____ _____ _____ _____ time heals all wounds.

시간이 모든 상처를 치유한다고들 말한다.

3 If you _____ _____, I'll take your word for it.

네가 그렇게 말한다면 나는 그것에 관한 네 말을 믿을 것이다.

4 She seemed to have _____ _____ _____.

그녀는 무언가 할 말이 있어 보였다.

Word Box | talent 몝 재능   wound 몝 부상, 상처 됭 상처 입히다   take one's word ~의 말을 믿다

Ⓐ **Expressions** 표현을 듣고, 큰 소리로 세 번씩 읽어 보세요.

MP3-071

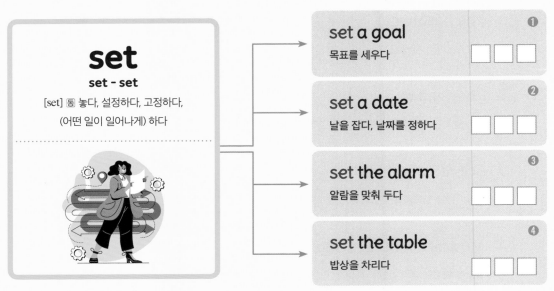

set
set – set
[set] 통 놓다, 설정하다, 고정하다,
(어떤 일이 일어나게) 하다

❶ set a goal
목표를 세우다 ☐☐☐

❷ set a date
날을 잡다, 날짜를 정하다 ☐☐☐

❸ set the alarm
알람을 맞춰 두다 ☐☐☐

❹ set the table
밥상을 차리다 ☐☐☐

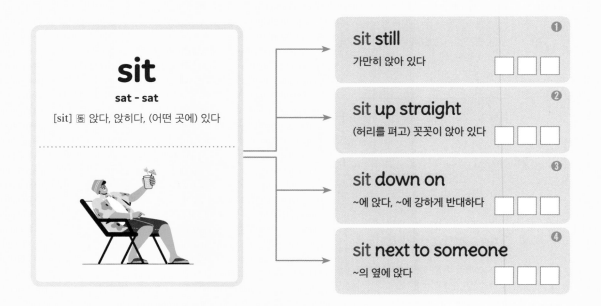

sit
sat – sat
[sit] 통 앉다, 앉히다, (어떤 곳에) 있다

❶ sit still
가만히 앉아 있다 ☐☐☐

❷ sit up straight
(허리를 펴고) 꼿꼿이 앉아 있다 ☐☐☐

❸ sit down on
~에 앉다, ~에 강하게 반대하다 ☐☐☐

❹ sit next to someone
~의 옆에 앉다 ☐☐☐

⑧ Check the Expressions

문장을 듣고, 빈칸에 알맞은 단어를 써 보세요.

MP3-072

set

1 People often _____ _____ _____ on New Year's Day.

사람들은 흔히 새해 첫날 목표를 세운다.

2 We _____ _____ _____ for Gildong's birthday party.

우리는 길동의 생일파티 날짜를 정했다.

3 I _____ _____ _____ before I go to bed.

나는 잠자기 전에 알람을 맞춰 놓는다.

4 The kids helped their mom _____ _____ _____.

아이들은 엄마가 식탁 차리는 것을 도왔다.

sit

1 I was so excited that I couldn't _____ _____.

나는 너무 신이 나서 가만히 앉아 있지 못했다.

2 My mom always tells me to _____ _____ _____.

우리 엄마는 항상 허리를 펴고 꼿꼿이 앉으라고 말씀하신다.

3 She asked the children to _____ _____ _____ the chairs.

그녀는 아이들에게 의자에 앉으라고 요청했다.

4 Jisoo usually _____ _____ _____ _____ in math class.

지수는 수학 시간에 보통 내 옆에 앉는다.

Word Box | still 형 가만히 있는, 고요한, 정지한 straight 부 똑바로, 곧장 형 똑바른, 곧은

A 우리말 뜻에 맞게 단어들을 연결하세요.

1 도망치다   run •   • so

2 그렇게 말하다   say •   • a goal

3 목표를 세우다   set •   • down on

4 ~에 앉다   sit •   • away

B <보기>에 주어진 단어를 이용하여 우리말 뜻에 맞게 문장을 완성해 보세요. (수 일치와 시제에 주의하세요.)

보기	set say sit run

1 A sense of humor seems to _____ in my family.

유머 감각은 우리 집안 내력인 것 같다.

2 Edison seemed to have something to _____.

에디슨은 무언가 할 말이 있어 보였다.

3 She asked me to _____ the table for dinner.

그녀는 나에게 저녁 밥상을 차려 달라고 부탁했다.

4 He was so nervous that he couldn't _____ still.

그는 너무 긴장해서 가만히 앉아 있지 못했다.

C 다음 문장의 빈칸에 공통으로 들어가는 단어를 써 보세요.

1 They _____ a date for the appointment.

I _____ the alarm for 7 a.m. to wake up early.

[   ]

2 Remember to _____ up straight and stay attentive.

They usually _____ next to me during class.

[   ]

D 다음 문장에서 틀린 부분을 찾아 바르게 고쳐 써 보세요.

1 They had to run at their lives to find shelter.

→ _____

2 It is say that time heals all wounds.

→ _____

3 People often setting a goal on New Year's Day.

→ _____

4 She asked the children to sat down at the chairs.

→ _____

Ⓐ Expressions 표현을 듣고, 큰 소리로 세 번씩 읽어 보세요.

MP3-073

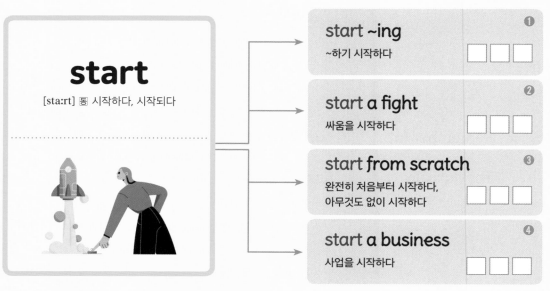

start

[staːrt] 图 시작하다, 시작되다

❶ start ~ing
~하기 시작하다

❷ start a fight
싸움을 시작하다

❸ start from scratch
완전히 처음부터 시작하다,
아무것도 없이 시작하다

❹ start a business
사업을 시작하다

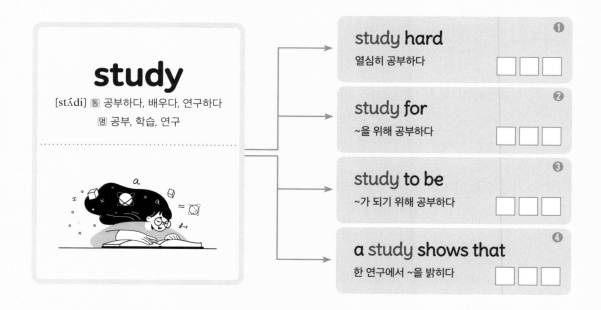

study

[stʌ́di] 图 공부하다, 배우다, 연구하다
명 공부, 학습, 연구

❶ study hard
열심히 공부하다

❷ study for
~을 위해 공부하다

❸ study to be
~가 되기 위해 공부하다

❹ a study shows that
한 연구에서 ~을 밝히다

Ⓑ Check the Expressions

문장을 듣고, 빈칸에 알맞은 단어를 써 보세요.

MP3-074

start

1 We _____ _____ online learning platforms.

우리는 온라인 학습 플랫폼을 사용하기 시작했다.

2 He decided to _____ _____ _____ with a betrayer.

그는 배신자와 싸움을 시작하기로 결심했다.

3 After the disaster, they had to _____ _____ _____.

재난을 겪은 후 그들은 완전히 처음부터 다시 시작해야 했다.

4 I want to _____ my own _____ someday.

나는 언젠가 나의 사업을 시작하고 싶다.

study

1 If you _____ _____, you'll get a good grade.

공부를 열심히 하면 좋은 성적을 받을 것이다.

2 She helped me _____ _____ the midterm.

그녀는 내가 중간고사 공부하는 것을 도와주었다.

3 He should _____ _____ _____ a doctor.

그는 의사가 되기 위해 공부해야 한다.

4 _____ _____ _____ _____ eating breakfast is good for your health.

한 연구에 의하면 아침을 먹는 것이 건강에 좋다고 한다.

Word Box | betrayer 명 배신자 disaster 명 재난, 참사 midterm 명 중간고사 형 한 학기 중간의

Ⓐ Expressions 표현을 듣고, 큰 소리로 세 번씩 읽어 보세요.

MP3-075

talk

[tɔːk] 통 말하다, 이야기하다, 대화하다

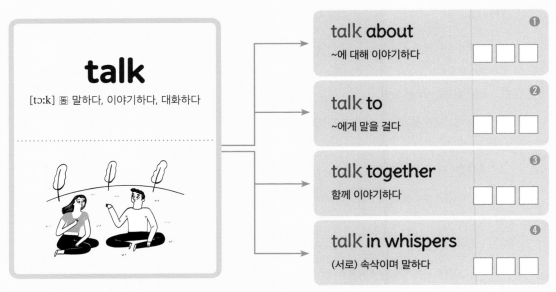

❶ **talk about**
~에 대해 이야기하다

❷ **talk to**
~에게 말을 걸다

❸ **talk together**
함께 이야기하다

❹ **talk in whispers**
(서로) 속삭이며 말하다

tell

told - told

[tel] 통 말하다, 알리다, 구별하다, 알다

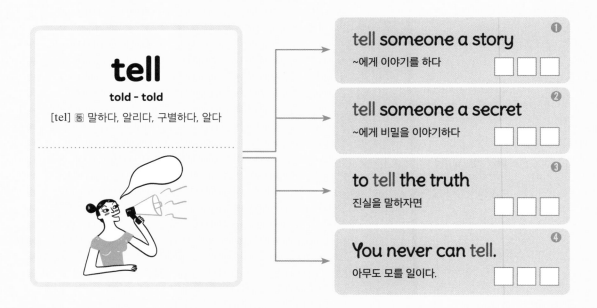

❶ **tell someone a story**
~에게 이야기를 하다

❷ **tell someone a secret**
~에게 비밀을 이야기하다

❸ **to tell the truth**
진실을 말하자면

❹ **You never can tell.**
아무도 모를 일이다.

Ⓑ Check the Expressions

문장을 듣고, 빈칸에 알맞은 단어를 써 보세요.

talk

1 They always love to _____ _____ soccer.

그들은 항상 축구에 관해 이야기하는 것을 좋아한다.

2 I'm busy right now, but I'll _____ _____ you later.

지금은 내가 바쁘니 나중에 이야기하자.

3 It's important for team members to _____ _____.

팀 구성원들이 함께 이야기하는 것이 중요하다.

4 The children _____ _____ _____ during the game.

아이들은 게임을 하는 동안 귓속말을 했다.   ★ He ~~told~~ about his childhood. (X) talked about (O)

tell

1 She _____ _____ _____ _____ about summer camp.

그녀는 우리에게 여름 캠프에 대한 이야기를 했다.

2 My friend _____ _____ _____ _____.

내 친구는 나에게 비밀을 이야기했다.

3 _____ _____ _____ _____, I didn't like the movie.

사실대로 말하자면, 나는 그 영화를 별로 좋아하지 않았다.

4 _____ _____ _____ _____ which team will win this season.

이번 시즌에 어떤 팀이 이길지 아무도 모를 일이다.

> **Word Box** | whisper 몡 속삭임 통 속삭이다, 귓속말을 하다 season 몡 (1년 중 특정 활동이 있는) 시즌, 철

A 우리말 뜻에 맞게 단어들을 연결하세요.

1 완전히 처음부터 시작하다   start   •   • hard

2 열심히 공부하다   study   •   • from scratch

3 함께 이야기하다   talk   •   • the truth

4 진실을 말하자면   to tell   •   • together

B <보기>에 주어진 단어를 이용하여 우리말 뜻에 맞게 문장을 완성해 보세요. (수 일치와 시제에 주의하세요.)

> 보기   start   talk   study   tell

1 She took a loan from the bank to _____ her own business.

그녀는 자신의 사업을 시작하기 위해 은행에서 융자를 얻었다.

2 I am _____ to be an engineer.

나는 엔지니어가 되기 위해 공부하고 있다.

3 We love to _____ about our favorite actors.

우리는 좋아하는 배우들에 관해 이야기하는 것을 좋아한다.

4 She _____ us a story about her childhood.

그녀는 우리에게 자기 어린 시절 이야기를 했다.

C 다음 문장의 빈칸에 공통으로 들어가는 단어를 써 보세요.

1 It's not worth it to _____ a fight over that matter.

   After the war, they had to _____ from scratch.

   [   ]

2 We _____ together to find a solution.

   They _____ in whispers to avoid being overheard.

   [   ]

D 다음 문장에서 틀린 부분을 찾아 바르게 고쳐 써 보세요.

1 We started use online learning platforms.

   → _____

2 She helped me to study to the midterm.

   → _____

3 The children talked whisper during the game.

   → _____

4 My friend told to me a secret.

   → _____

Unit 14 think / try / turn / wait

Ⓐ Expressions 표현을 듣고, 큰 소리로 세 번씩 읽어 보세요.

MP3-077

think
thought - thought
[θiŋk] 동 생각하다, ~일 것 같다,
(~라고) 믿다

❶ **think hard**
골똘히 생각하다

❷ **think twice**
재고하다, 망설이다

❸ **think straight**
명쾌하게[논리적으로] 생각하다

❹ **think big**
넓게 생각하다

try
[trai] 동 노력하다, 애쓰다, ~하려고 시도하다
명 시도, 노력

❶ **try one's best**
최선을 다하다

❷ **try something new**
새로운 것에 도전하다

❸ **try hard**
열심히 노력하다

❹ **be worth a try**
시도해 볼 만한 가치가 있다

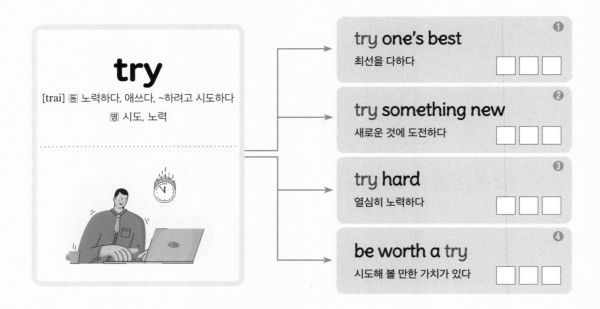

Ⓑ Check the Expressions

문장을 듣고, 빈칸에 알맞은 단어를 써 보세요.

think

1 She _____ very _____ before deciding it.

그녀는 그것을 결정하기 전에 아주 골똘히 생각했다.

2 It's wise to _____ _____ whether it's good for you.

그것이 너에게 좋은 일인지 재고해 보는 것이 현명하다.

3 _____ _____ before responding to the question.

질문에 대답하기 전에 논리적으로 생각하세요.

4 The teachers encouraged children to _____ _____.

선생님들은 아이들이 넓게 생각하도록 격려했다.

⭐ A: Do you think he will come?
B: I think it. (X) I think so. (O)

try

1 You won't regret if you _____ _____ _____.

최선을 다한다면 너는 후회하지 않을 것이다.

2 She always enjoys _____ _____ _____.

그녀는 항상 새로운 것에 도전하는 것을 즐긴다.

3 I _____ _____ to break my bad habit.

나는 나쁜 버릇을 고치기 위해 열심히 노력했다.

4 Learning a new language _____ _____ _____ _____.

새로운 언어를 배우는 것은 시도할 가치가 있다.

Word Box | worth 형 ~의 가치가 있는 encourage 동 격려하다, 용기를 북돋우다 habit 명 버릇, 습관

think / try / turn / wait

Ⓐ Expressions 표현을 듣고, 큰 소리로 세 번씩 읽어 보세요.

MP3-079

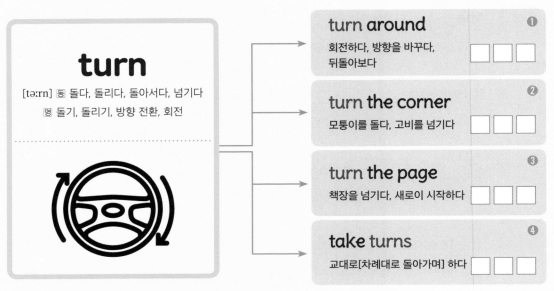

turn

[təːrn] 동 돌다, 돌리다, 돌아서다, 넘기다
명 돌기, 돌리기, 방향 전환, 회전

turn around ❶
회전하다, 방향을 바꾸다, 뒤돌아보다

turn the corner ❷
모퉁이를 돌다, 고비를 넘기다

turn the page ❸
책장을 넘기다, 새로이 시작하다

take turns ❹
교대로[차례대로 돌아가며] 하다

wait

[weit] 동 기다리다

wait for ❶
~을 기다리다

wait long ❷
오래 기다리다

wait patiently ❸
인내심을 가지고 기다리다

can't wait ❹
기다릴 수 없다, 빨리 ~하고 싶다

Ⓑ Check the Expressions

문장을 듣고, 빈칸에 알맞은 단어를 써 보세요.

MP3-080

turn

1 She _____ _____ waving her hands.

그녀는 손을 흔들며 돌아섰다.

2 I _____ _____ _____ and found the bank.

나는 길 모퉁이를 돌아서 은행을 발견했다.

3 It's time to _____ _____ _____.

새롭게 시작해야 될 때이다.

4 We _____ _____ while playing a board game.

우리는 보드게임을 할 때 차례대로 했다.

wait

1 Many people were _____ _____ their turns.

많은 사람이 자기 차례를 기다리고 있었다.

⭐ I ~~waited~~ my turn. (X)

2 We had to _____ _____ at the restaurant.

우리는 식당에서 오래도록 기다려야 했다.

3 I _____ _____ for the response to my email.

나는 이메일에 대한 답장을 인내심을 가지고 기다렸다.

4 I _____ _____ to sleep in and recharge.

나는 빨리 자고 에너지를 회복하고 싶다.

Word Box | patiently 🈁 참을성 있게   wave 🈁 (손, 팔을) 흔들다   recharge 🈁 충전하다, (휴식으로) 재충전하다

A 우리말 뜻에 맞게 단어들을 연결하세요.

1	재고하다, 망설이다	think •	• one's best
2	최선을 다하다	try •	• the corner
3	모퉁이를 돌다	turn •	• twice
4	오래 기다리다	wait •	• long

B <보기>에 주어진 단어를 이용하여 우리말 뜻에 맞게 문장을 완성해 보세요. (수 일치와 시제에 주의하세요.)

보기
turn   wait   think   try

1 I had to _____ hard to come up with an answer.
나는 정답을 찾아내기 위해 열심히 생각해야 했다.

2 He always enjoys _____ something new.
그는 항상 새로운 것에 도전하는 것을 즐긴다.

3 She _____ around to go home.
그녀는 집으로 가기 위해 돌아섰다.

4 I _____ patiently for the text message from my friend.
나는 친구의 문자 메시지를 인내심을 가지고 기다렸다.

다음 문장의 빈칸에 공통으로 들어가는 단어를 써 보세요.

1 It's important to _____ twice before you make a decision.

You should _____ straight and consider all the facts.

2 You won't regret if you _____ your very best.

If you want to succeed, you have to _____ hard.

D 다음 문장에서 틀린 부분을 찾아 바르게 고쳐 써 보세요.

1 Think straightly before responding to the question.

→ _____

2 Learning a new language is worth try.

→ _____

3 We took turn while playing a board game.

→ _____

4 Many people were waiting to their turns.

→ _____

Ⓐ Expressions 표현을 듣고, 큰 소리로 세 번씩 읽어 보세요.

MP3-081

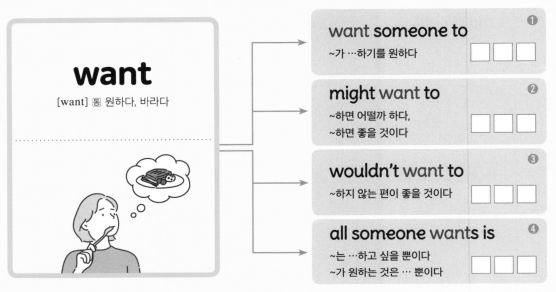

want

[want] 통 원하다, 바라다

❶ **want someone to**
~가 …하기를 원하다 ☐☐☐

❷ **might want to**
~하면 어떨까 하다,
~하면 좋을 것이다 ☐☐☐

❸ **wouldn't want to**
~하지 않는 편이 좋을 것이다 ☐☐☐

❹ **all someone wants is**
~는 …하고 싶을 뿐이다
~가 원하는 것은 … 뿐이다 ☐☐☐

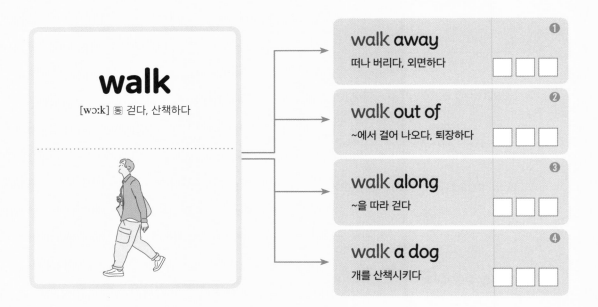

walk

[wɔːk] 통 걷다, 산책하다

❶ **walk away**
떠나 버리다, 외면하다 ☐☐☐

❷ **walk out of**
~에서 걸어 나오다, 퇴장하다 ☐☐☐

❸ **walk along**
~을 따라 걷다 ☐☐☐

❹ **walk a dog**
개를 산책시키다 ☐☐☐

ⒷCheck the Expressions

문장을 듣고, 빈칸에 알맞은 단어를 써 보세요.

MP3-082

want

1 They _____ _____ _____ join their team.

그들은 내가 팀에 합류하기를 원했다.

2 You _____ _____ _____ bring an umbrella with you.

너는 우산을 가져가는 게 좋을 것 같다.

3 You _____ _____ _____ watch that movie.

너는 그 영화를 보지 않는 것이 좋을 것이다.

4 _____ _____ _____ _____ to go on a trip with my friends.

나는 친구들과 여행을 가고 싶을 뿐이다.   ⭐ I am wanting some ice cream. (X) I want ~ (O)

walk

1 Don't _____ _____ when you find difficulties.

어려움이 생겼을 때 외면하지 마세요.

2 They _____ _____ _____ the crowds.

그들은 군중 속에서 걸어 나왔다.

3 We used to _____ _____ the river.

우리는 강을 따라 걷곤 했다.

4 I carry waste bags when I _____ my _____.

나는 개를 산책 시킬 때 쓰레기 봉투를 가지고 다닌다.

> **Word Box** | difficulty 몡 어려움   crowd 몡 군중   waste 몡 쓰레기, 낭비, 불모지

want / walk / watch / win

Ⓐ Expressions 표현을 듣고, 큰 소리로 세 번씩 읽어 보세요.

MP3-083

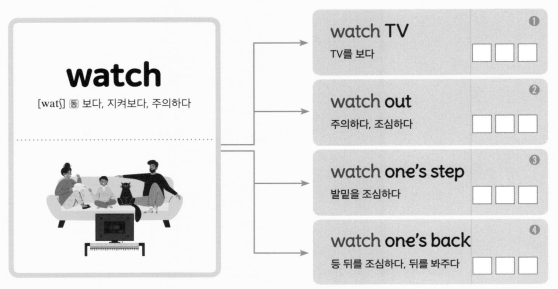

watch

[watʃ] 동 보다, 지켜보다, 주의하다

❶ **watch TV**
TV를 보다 ☐☐☐

❷ **watch out**
주의하다, 조심하다 ☐☐☐

❸ **watch one's step**
발밑을 조심하다 ☐☐☐

❹ **watch one's back**
등 뒤를 조심하다, 뒤를 봐주다 ☐☐☐

win
won - won
[win] 동 이기다, 따다

❶ **win a game**
경기에서 이기다 ☐☐☐

❷ **win a race**
경주에서 이기다 ☐☐☐

❸ **win a war**
전쟁에서 이기다 ☐☐☐

❹ **win an election**
선거에서 이기다 ☐☐☐

ⓑ Check the Expressions

문장을 듣고, 빈칸에 알맞은 단어를 써 보세요.

watch

1 We gathered to _____ _____ together.

우리는 모여서 TV를 봤다.

⭐ I see TV. (X) I look TV. (X)

2 _____ _____ for the slippery floor.

미끄러운 바닥을 조심하세요.

3 _____ _____ _____ and take it slowly.

발밑을 조심하고 천천히 걸으세요.

4 _____ _____ _____ and stay alert.

뒤를 조심하고 경계를 늦추지 마세요.

win

1 I hope we will _____ _____ _____.

나는 우리가 시합에서 이기기를 희망한다.

2 They're trying to _____ _____ _____.

그들은 경주에서 이기기 위해 노력한다.

3 He played a role in _____ the _____.

그가 그 전쟁에서 이기는 데 역할을 했다.

4 I wonder who will _____ the _____.

나는 누가 그 선거에서 이길지 궁금하다.

Word Box | election 몡 선거 slippery 혱 미끄러운 alert 혱 경계하는 통 알리다, 경보를 발하다

A   우리말 뜻에 맞게 단어들을 연결하세요.

1   ~하면 좋을 것이다   might   •   • want to

2   개를 산책 시키다   walk   •   • out

3   주의하다   watch   •   • an election

4   선거에서 이기다   win   •   • a dog

B   <보기>에 주어진 단어를 이용하여 우리말 뜻에 맞게 문장을 완성해 보세요. (수 일치와 시제에 주의하세요.)

<보기> want   walk   watch   win

1   They _____ me to go with them.

그들은 내가 그들과 함께 가기를 원했다.

2   We held hands and _____ along the beach.

우리는 손을 잡고 해변을 따라 걸었다.

3   You need to _____ your back and stay away from gossip.

뒤를 조심하고 험담을 멀리해야 한다.

4   He played a role in _____ the war.

그가 그 전쟁에서 이기는 데 역할을 했다.

C 다음 문장의 빈칸에 공통으로 들어가는 단어를 써 보세요.

1 Don't _____ away when someone needs your help.

  We used to _____ along the park trail.

  [   ]

2 I like to relax and _____ TV after school.

  Be sure to _____ your step while climbing.

  [   ]

D 다음 문장에서 틀린 부분을 찾아 바르게 고쳐 써 보세요.

1 All I wanting is to go on a trip with my friends.

  → _____

2 They walked out the crowds.

  → _____

3 Watch with your back and stay alert.

  → _____

4 They're trying to winning about a race.

  → _____

Expression Check List

➜ 아는 표현 앞에 √ 표시를 해 보세요. 기억나지 않는 표현은 다시 확인해 암기하세요.

√	표현	√	표현
	receive an award		would say
	receive an invitation		it is said that
	receive visitors		say so
	receive treatment		something to say
	remember well		set a goal
	remember to		set a date
	hardly remember		set the alarm
	as far as someone remembers		set the table
	respect for		sit still
	respect one's privacy		sit up straight
	respect human rights		sit down on
	deserve respect		sit next to someone
	return to		start ~ing
	return from		start a fight
	return one's call		start from scratch
	return the favor		start a business
	run away		study hard
	run for one's life		study for
	run some tests		study to be
	run in one's family		a study shows that

√	표현	√	표현
	talk about		wait for
	talk to		wait long
	talk together		wait patiently
	talk in whispers		can't wait
	tell someone a story		want someone to
	tell someone a secret		might want to
	to tell the truth		wouldn't want to
	You never can tell.		all someone wants is
	think hard		walk away
	think twice		walk out of
	think straight		walk along
	think big		walk a dog
	try one's best		watch TV
	try something new		watch out
	try hard		watch one's step
	be worth a try		watch one's back
	turn around		win a game
	turn the corner		win a race
	turn the page		win a war
	take turns		win an election

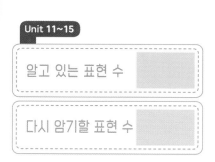

Unit 11~15

알고 있는 표현 수

다시 암기할 표현 수

Chapter 3

형용사와
영어표현

Ⓐ **Expressions** 표현을 듣고, 큰 소리로 세 번씩 읽어 보세요.

MP3-085

bad

[bæd] 형 나쁜, 안 좋은, 불쾌한

❶ bad **habit**
나쁜 습관, 나쁜 버릇

❷ bad **mood**
불쾌한 기분

❸ bad **temper**
참을성 없고 조급한
[화를 잘 내는] 성격

❹ **go** bad
썩다, 상하다, 나빠지다

big

[big] 형 큰, 나이가 더 많은, 성장한

❶ big **deal**
큰 일, 대수로운 일

❷ big **disappointment**
크게 실망스러운 일

❸ big **mistake**
큰 실수

❹ big **surprise**
크게 놀랄 만한 일

Ⓑ Check the Expressions

문장을 듣고, 빈칸에 알맞은 단어를 써 보세요.

bad

1 Smoking is a _____ _____ that can lead to addiction.

흡연은 중독이 될 수 있는 나쁜 습관이다.

2 She woke up in a _____ _____.

그녀는 불쾌한 기분으로 잠에서 깼다.

3 He's known for his _____ _____ and often gets angry.

그는 욱하는 성질로 유명하고 자주 화를 낸다.

4 I found that the yogurt had _____ _____.

나는 요거트가 상한 것을 발견했다.

big ⭐ It was in the ~~blue big~~ box. (X) It was in the big blue box. (O)

1 Winning the championship was a _____ _____ for us.

선수권 대회에서 이기는 것은 우리에게 대단히 중요한 일이었다.

2 Losing a job was a _____ _____.

실직하는 것은 크게 실망스러운 일이었다.

3 I made a _____ _____ by not listening to you.

나는 네 말을 듣지 않아서 큰 실수를 했다.

4 It was a _____ _____ to see you there.

너를 거기에서 본 것은 매우 놀랄 일이었다.

Word Box | temper 몡 성질, 성미 disappointment 몡 실망, 낙심 addiction 몡 중독

Ⓐ **Expressions** 표현을 듣고, 큰 소리로 세 번씩 읽어 보세요.

MP3-087

bright

[brait] 혱 (빛이) 밝은, 눈부신, 선명한

❶ bright **color**
밝은 색상

❷ bright **future**
밝은 미래

❸ bright **idea**
번뜩이는[기발한] 생각

❹ bright **side**
밝은[긍정적인] 면

chilly

[tʃíli] 혱 쌀쌀한, 추운, 냉랭한, 쌀쌀맞은

❶ chilly **morning**
쌀쌀한 아침

❷ chilly **air**
냉기, 쌀쌀한 공기

❸ chilly **wind**
찬 바람

❹ chilly **weather**
쌀쌀한[으스스한] 날씨

Ⓑ Check the Expressions

문장을 듣고, 빈칸에 알맞은 단어를 써 보세요.

MP3-088

bright

1 She bought a new dress in a _____ _____.

그녀는 밝은 색의 새 원피스를 샀다.

2 The advanced technology promises a _____ _____.

발전된 기술은 밝은 미래를 약속해 준다.

3 She came up with a _____ _____ for the group activity.

그녀는 모둠 활동을 위해 기발한 생각을 해냈다.

4 We always look on the _____ _____ of life.

우리는 항상 인생을 긍정적으로 본다.

chilly

★ chilly 쌀쌀한 〈 cold 추운 〈 freezing 매섭게 추운

1 It was a _____ _____, and I put on a sweater.

쌀쌀한 아침이어서 나는 스웨터를 입었다.

2 The _____ _____ carried the scent of fallen leaves.

쌀쌀한 공기가 낙엽의 냄새를 실어왔다.

3 They had to walk against the _____ _____.

그들은 찬 바람을 맞으며 걸어야 했다.

4 Stepping outside, I could feel the _____ _____.

밖으로 나가자 나는 으스스한 날씨를 느낄 수 있었다.

Word Box | advanced 형 선진의, 발전된   scent 명 향기

A ⓐ와 ⓑ에서 알맞은 단어를 하나씩 골라 표현을 완성하고, 우리말 뜻을 써 보세요.

ⓐ	ⓑ
bad big bright chilly	air disappointment color habit

1	bad	habit	_____
2			큰 실망
3			_____
4			_____

B 주어진 단어를 빈칸에 알맞게 배열하여 문장을 완성해 보세요.

1 He woke up _____ due to a stomachache.
   (a / in / mood / bad)

2 Winning the final was _____.
   (a / deal / us / big / for)

3 I always look on _____ every situation.
   (the / side / of / bright)

4 We had to walk _____.
   (chilly / the / wind / against)

C 문장의 빈칸에 우리말 뜻에 맞는 표현을 써 보세요.

1 He's known for his _____ _____ and often gets angry.

　　　　　　　　　　　　　욱하는 성질

2 It was a _____ _____ to see you there.

　　　　　　　크게 놀라운 일

3 She came up with a _____ _____ for the group activity.

　　　　　　　　　　　　　　　기발한 생각

4 It was a _____ _____, and I put on a sweater.

　　　　　　　쌀쌀한 아침

D 다음 글의 빈칸에 알맞은 표현을 우리말 뜻을 보고 써 보세요.

1
> You are all capable of creating a _____ _____ for
>
　　　　　　　　　　　　　　　　　　　　　밝은 미래
> yourselves. However, it's important to learn from your mistakes
> along the way. Making a _____ _____ doesn't mean it's
>
　　　　　　　　　　　　　　　큰 실수
> the end of the world.

2
> When the _____ _____ arrives, make sure to dress warmly
>
　　　　　　　쌀쌀한 날씨
> to stay cozy and comfortable. Remember, even when the weather
> is cold, it doesn't mean your day has to _____ _____.
>
　　　　　　　　　　　　　　　　　　　　　　　　나빠지다

Ⓐ Expressions 표현을 듣고, 큰 소리로 세 번씩 읽어 보세요.

MP3-089

clear
[kliər] 형 쉬운, 분명한, 확실한

❶ clear message
명확한 메시지 ☐☐☐

❷ clear understanding
확실한 이해 ☐☐☐

❸ make something clear
~을 분명하게 하다 ☐☐☐

❹ crystal clear
명명백백한, 아주 분명한 ☐☐☐

common
[káːmən] 형 흔한, 공통의, 공동의

❶ common language
공용어 ☐☐☐

❷ common knowledge
상식 ☐☐☐

❸ common name
흔한 이름 ☐☐☐

❹ common enemy
공공의 적 ☐☐☐

Ⓑ Check the Expressions

문장을 듣고, 빈칸에 알맞은 단어를 써 보세요.

clear ★ clear 무색의 깨끗한 I transparent 투명한 I see-through 속이 보이는 (주로 의류에 사용)

1 He gave a _____ _____ to the audience.

그는 청중들에게 명확한 메시지를 전달했다.

2 We need to have a _____ _____ of our rights.

우리는 우리의 권리에 대한 확실한 이해가 필요하다.

3 Using visual aids can _____ _____ _____.

시각적 보조 장치들을 사용하면 그것을 명확하게 볼 수 있다.

4 The mountain lake was _____ _____.

산속의 호수는 매우 맑았다.

common

1 English is often used as a _____ _____.

영어는 자주 공용어로 사용된다.

2 It is _____ _____ that water boils at 100 degrees.

물이 100도에서 끓는다는 것은 상식이다.

3 "John" is a very _____ _____ in the U.S.

'존'은 미국에서 매우 흔한 이름이다.

4 The superheroes defeated their _____ _____.

슈퍼 영웅들이 그들의 공공의 적을 무찔렀다.

Word Box | audience 명 청중 visual 형 시각의 aid 명 보조 기구 degree 명 (각도·온도의) 도 defeat 동 무찌르다

Ⓐ Expressions 표현을 듣고, 큰 소리로 세 번씩 읽어 보세요.

MP3-091

deep
[diːp] 형 깊은, 심각한

❶ deep sleep
깊은 잠 ☐☐☐

❷ deep trouble
심각한 곤경 ☐☐☐

❸ deep thought
깊은 생각, 심사숙고 ☐☐☐

❹ deep breath
심호흡 ☐☐☐

direct
[dirékt, dai-] 형 직접적인, 직행의

❶ direct flight
직항편 ☐☐☐

❷ direct quote
직접적인 인용문 ☐☐☐

❸ direct experience
직접 경험 ☐☐☐

❹ direct message
직접 메시지(=DM) ☐☐☐

ⓑ Check the Expressions

문장을 듣고, 빈칸에 알맞은 단어를 써 보세요.

deep

1 The princess fell into a _____ _____.

공주는 깊은 잠에 빠졌다.

2 I think you're in _____ _____.

너 큰일 난 거 같다.

⭐ 심각한 곤경: big[serious, deep] trouble

3 Looking out the window, she was lost in _____ _____.

창 밖을 바라보며 그녀는 깊은 생각에 빠졌다.

4 Take a _____ _____ of fresh air and clear your mind.

신선한 공기를 깊게 들이마시고 마음을 비우세요.

direct

1 She booked a _____ _____ to New York.

그녀는 뉴욕행 직항편을 예약했다.

2 You'd better use a _____ _____ from the book.

책에서 직접 인용문을 사용하는 것이 더 나을 것이다.

3 People learn better through _____ _____.

사람들은 직접적인 경험에서 더 잘 배운다.

4 We can send a _____ _____ to our followers.

우리는 팔로워들에게 DM(직접 메시지)을 보낼 수 있다.

Word Box | quote 몡 인용문(=quotation) 동 인용하다 follower 몡 추종자, 팬, (블로그 등의) 팔로워

A ⓐ와 ⓑ에서 알맞은 단어를 하나씩 골라 표현을 완성하고, 우리말 뜻을 써 보세요.

ⓐ	ⓑ
crystal common deep direct	enemy clear trouble message

1 [_____ | _____] _____

2 [_____ | _____] _____

3 [_____ | _____] _____

4 [_____ | _____] _____

B 주어진 단어를 빈칸에 알맞게 배열하여 문장을 완성해 보세요.

1 Using visual aids can _____.
   (make / clear / it)

2 _____ that water freezes at 0 degrees.
   (is / common / It / knowledge)

3 _____ and relax your body.
   (Take / deep / a / breath)

4 We can learn better _____.
   (direct / through / experience)

C 문장의 빈칸에 우리말 뜻에 맞는 표현을 써 보세요.

1 We need to have a _____ _____ of our rights.
분명한 이해

2 "John" is a very _____ _____ in the U.S.
흔한 이름

3 She was lost in _____ _____.
깊은 생각

4 You'd better use a _____ _____ from the book.
직접 인용문

D 다음 글의 빈칸에 알맞은 표현을 우리말 뜻을 보고 써 보세요.

1
> After a long day of playing outside, the little girl fell into a _____ _____, dreaming of magical adventures. The
> 깊은 잠
> next day, her family surprised her with a _____ _____ to a
> 직항 비행편
> theme park. She boarded the plane, ready for a real-life adventure.

2
> People from different backgrounds came together to trade goods and share stories. To communicate effectively, they needed a _____ _____ that everyone understood. English allowed
> 공용 언어
> them to exchange ideas and deliver a _____ _____.
> 명확한 메시지

early / easy / empty / excellent

Ⓐ Expressions 표현을 듣고, 큰 소리로 세 번씩 읽어 보세요.

MP3-093

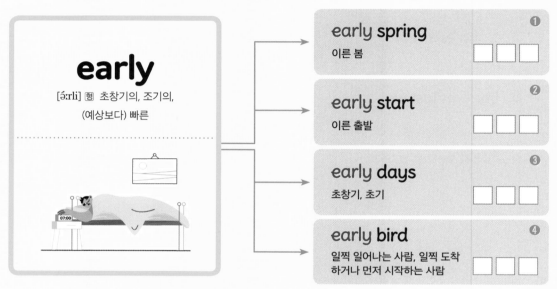

early
[ə́ːrli] 형 초창기의, 조기의,
(예상보다) 빠른

early spring ❶
이른 봄

early start ❷
이른 출발

early days ❸
초창기, 초기

early bird ❹
일찍 일어나는 사람, 일찍 도착
하거나 먼저 시작하는 사람

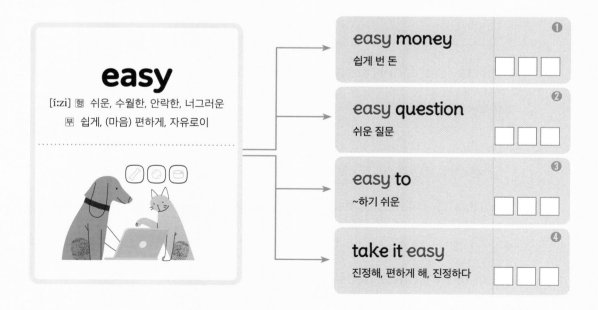

easy
[íːzi] 형 쉬운, 수월한, 안락한, 너그러운
부 쉽게, (마음) 편하게, 자유로이

easy money ❶
쉽게 번 돈

easy question ❷
쉬운 질문

easy to ❸
~하기 쉬운

take it easy ❹
진정해, 편하게 해, 진정하다

Ⓑ Check the Expressions

문장을 듣고, 빈칸에 알맞은 단어를 써 보세요.

early

1 Colorful flowers bloom in _____ _____.

형형색색의 꽃들이 이른 봄에 피어난다.

2 She decided to get an _____ _____ on her homework.

그녀는 숙제를 일찍 시작하기로 결심했다.

3 Back in the _____ _____ of photography, cameras used film rolls.

사진술 초창기에는 카메라에 필름을 사용했다.

4 The _____ _____ got the best seat at the concert.

일찍 가는 사람이 콘서트에서 좋은 자리를 차지했다.

easy

1 He realized that there's no such thing as _____ _____.

그는 세상에 쉽게 벌 수 있는 돈이란 없다는 것을 깨달았다.

2 Luckily, the quiz had many _____ _____.

다행스럽게도 쪽지 시험에는 쉬운 문제가 많았다.

3 It was _____ _____ understand the online tutorial.

온라인 사용 지침서를 이해하는 것은 쉬웠다.

4 _____ _____ _____ and give yourself a break.

진정하시고, 좀 쉬면서 하세요.

Word Box | photography 명 사진술, 사진 촬영   tutorial 명 사용 지침서, 지도서

early / easy / empty / excellent

Ⓐ Expressions 표현을 듣고, 큰 소리로 세 번씩 읽어 보세요.

MP3-095

empty
[émpti] 형 빈, 공허한, 무의미한

❶ empty space
빈 공간

❷ empty promise
공허한[거짓] 약속

❸ feel empty
공허하다, 허전하다

❹ empty-handed
빈손으로, 빈손인

excellent
[éksələnt] 형 뛰어난, 탁월한, 아주 좋아

❶ excellent job
잘한 일, 좋은 직업

❷ excellent grade
우수한 성적

❸ excellent condition
좋은 상태

❹ excellent choice
탁월한 선택

Ⓑ Check the Expressions

문장을 듣고, 빈칸에 알맞은 단어를 써 보세요.

empty

1 The parking lot had many _____ _____.

주차장에는 빈 자리가 많았다.

2 Parents should not make _____ _____.

부모들은 말 뿐인 약속들을 해서는 안 된다.

3 She couldn't help but _____ _____ inside.

그녀는 속으로 공허함을 느끼지 않을 수 없었다.

4 The explorers had to come back _____ - _____.

탐험가들은 빈손으로 돌아와야만 했다.

excellent

⭐ It's a ~~very~~ excellent idea. (X) excellent는 very와 함께 쓸 수 없음

1 You did an _____ _____ on your presentation.

너는 발표를 아주 잘했다.

2 He received _____ _____ in all subjects.

그는 모든 과목에서 뛰어난 성적을 받았다.

3 Her used bike was in _____ _____.

그녀의 중고 자전거는 상태가 좋았다.

4 You made an _____ _____ with your menu.

너는 메뉴를 아주 잘 골랐다.

Word Box | parking lot 명 주차장 explorer 명 탐험가 used 형 중고의

A ⓐ와 ⓑ에서 알맞은 단어를 하나씩 골라 표현을 완성하고, 우리말 뜻을 써 보세요.

ⓐ	ⓑ
early excellent empty easy	bird promise question grade

1 _____ _____ _____

2 _____ _____ _____

3 _____ _____ _____

4 _____ _____ _____

B 주어진 단어를 빈칸에 알맞게 배열하여 문장을 완성해 보세요.

1 Roses and lilies bloom _____.

   (early / in / spring)

2 It was _____ the teacher's instructions.

   (easy / understand / to)

3 They had to _____.

   (empty-handed / come / back)

4 Her used book was _____.

   (in / condition / excellent)

C 문장의 빈칸에 우리말 뜻에 맞는 표현을 써 보세요.

1 She decided to get an _____ _____ on her homework.
이른 시작

2 _____ _____ _____ and give yourself a break.
진정하다

3 She couldn't help but _____ _____ inside.
공허하다고 느끼다

4 You did an _____ _____ on your presentation.
잘한 일

D 다음 글의 빈칸에 알맞은 표현을 우리말 뜻을 보고 써 보세요.

1
In the _____ _____ of my career, I used to dream about
초창기
making _____ _____. I thought it would be simple and
쉽게 버는 돈
quick. But as I learned more, I realized that earning money requires

hard work and effort.

2
Emma's room was crowded with toys. She decided to organize

and create an _____ _____. It made her room feel bigger
빈 공간
and peaceful. It was an _____ _____ that made her happy
탁월한 선택
and proud of her decision.

Ⓐ Expressions 표현을 듣고, 큰 소리로 세 번씩 읽어 보세요.

MP3-097

full

[ful] 형 가득한, 완전한, 아주 많은

❶ **full name**
성명(성과 이름 모두) □ □ □

❷ **full moon**
보름달 □ □ □

❸ **full-time**
전업의, 상근의 □ □ □

❹ **full of energy**
활기가 넘치는 □ □ □

front

[frʌnt] 형 앞쪽의, 정면의
명 앞면, 앞쪽

❶ **front page**
1면 □ □ □

❷ **front seat**
앞 좌석 □ □ □

❸ **front row**
앞줄 □ □ □

❹ **in front of**
~의 앞에 □ □ □

Ⓑ Check the Expressions

문장을 듣고, 빈칸에 알맞은 단어를 써 보세요.

full

★ full 가득 찬 ‹ packed 꽉 찬 ‹ overloaded 꽉 차서 넘치는

1 You're supposed to write down your _____ _____.

너는 성과 이름 모두를 써야 한다.

2 We looked up at the _____ _____ and made a wish.

우리는 보름달을 올려다보며 소원을 빌었다.

3 He was offered a _____ - _____ job at the company.

그는 회사에서 정직원을 제안 받았다.

4 My little brother is always _____ _____ _____.

내 남동생은 항상 활기가 넘친다.

front

1 The story made the _____ _____ in all the newspapers.

그 이야기는 모든 신문의 1면에 실렸다.

2 I prefer sitting in the _____ _____.

나는 앞 좌석에 앉는 게 더 좋다.

3 You can see better in the _____ _____.

너는 앞줄에서 더 잘 볼 수 있다.

4 I often get nervous _____ _____ _____ a large audience.

나는 많은 관객 앞에서 긴장할 때가 많다.

Word Box | row 명 열, 줄 be supposed to ~하기로 되어있다, ~해야 한다, ~인 것으로 여겨진다

Ⓐ **Expressions** 표현을 듣고, 큰 소리로 세 번씩 읽어 보세요.

MP3-099

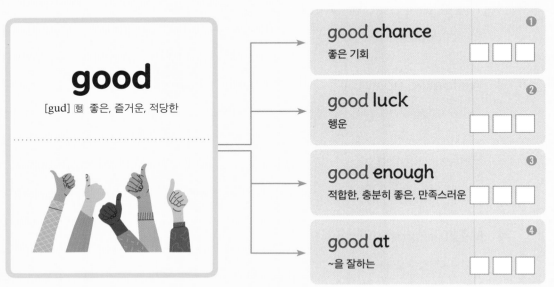

good

[gud] 형 좋은, 즐거운, 적당한

❶ good **chance**
좋은 기회

❷ good **luck**
행운

❸ good **enough**
적합한, 충분히 좋은, 만족스러운

❹ good **at**
~을 잘하는

great

[greit] 형 큰, 엄청난, 많은

❶ great **success**
대성공

❷ great **opportunity**
굉장한[멋진] 기회

❸ great **pride**
엄청난 자부심

❹ a great **deal of**
다량의, 많은

ⒷCheck the Expressions

문장을 듣고, 빈칸에 알맞은 단어를 써 보세요.

MP3-100

> **good**

1 It was a _____ _____ to see famous artworks.

그것은 유명한 미술 작품들을 볼 수 있는 좋은 기회였다.

2 I wish you _____ _____ in your new school.

새로운 학교에서 너에게 행운이 있기를 바란다.

3 Your explanation is simply not _____ _____.

네 설명이 충분하지 않을 뿐이다.

4 Sarah is _____ _____ playing the piano.

사라는 피아노를 잘 친다.

> **great**

⭐ He did a ~~very~~ great job. (X) great은 very와 함께 쓸 수 없음.
He did a very good job. (O)

1 We celebrated our _____ _____ in the school science fair.

우리는 교내 과학 박람회에서의 대성공을 축하했다.

2 It sounds like a _____ _____ to me.

그것은 나에겐 굉장한 기회인 것 같다.

3 She accepted the award with _____ _____.

그녀는 엄청난 자부심을 느끼며 상을 받았다.

4 Our team made _____ _____ _____ _____ progress.

우리 팀은 상당히 많은 발전을 이루었다.

Word Box artwork 명 미술[예술] 작품   fair 명 박람회, 전시회 형 좋은, 공정한

A ⓐ와 ⓑ에서 알맞은 단어를 하나씩 골라 표현을 완성하고, 우리말 뜻을 써 보세요.

ⓐ	ⓑ
full front good great	time enough row opportunity

1 _____   _____

2 _____   _____

3 _____   _____

4 _____   _____

B 주어진 단어를 빈칸에 알맞게 배열하여 문장을 완성해 보세요.

1 The children are always _____.

　　　　　　　　　　　(energy / full / of)

2 I often get worried _____ strangers.

　　　　　　　　　　　(front / in / of)

3 He _____ to improve my grade.

　　(gave / a / me / good / chance)

4 They spent _____ money on their vacation.

　　　　　　(a / deal / of / great)

C 문장의 빈칸에 우리말 뜻에 맞는 표현을 써 보세요.

1 You're supposed to write down your _____ _____.
성명

2 I prefer sitting in the _____ _____.
앞 좌석

3 Sarah is _____ _____ playing the piano.
~을 잘하다

4 She accepted the award with _____ _____.
대단한 자부심

D 다음 글의 빈칸에 알맞은 표현을 우리말 뜻을 보고 써 보세요.

1
During a clear night, a _____ _____ shines brightly in the
보름달
sky. Many people believe it brings _____ _____. They make
행운
wishes and hope for good things to happen.

2
On the _____ _____ of the newspaper, there was a big
1면
headline about their success. They were filled with joy and pride.
Everyone was excited to read the story of their _____ _____.
대성공

Ⓐ **Expressions** 표현을 듣고, 큰 소리로 세 번씩 읽어 보세요.

MP3-101

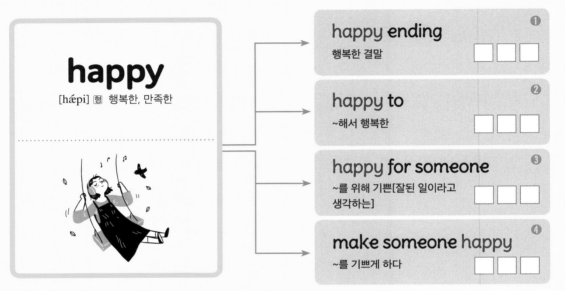

happy
[hǽpi] 형 행복한, 만족한

❶ **happy ending**
행복한 결말

❷ **happy to**
~해서 행복한

❸ **happy for someone**
~를 위해 기쁜[잘된 일이라고 생각하는]

❹ **make someone happy**
~를 기쁘게 하다

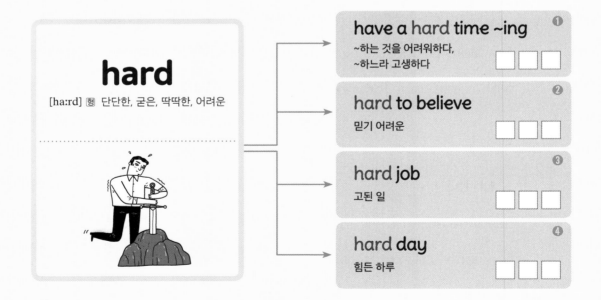

hard
[ha:rd] 형 단단한, 굳은, 딱딱한, 어려운

❶ **have a hard time ~ing**
~하는 것을 어려워하다,
~하느라 고생하다

❷ **hard to believe**
믿기 어려운

❸ **hard job**
고된 일

❹ **hard day**
힘든 하루

ⓑ Check the Expressions

문장을 듣고, 빈칸에 알맞은 단어를 써 보세요.

happy ⭐ I'm happy for you. (O) I'm happy ~~for being~~ here. (X) I'm happy to be here. (O)

1 The Cinderella story has a _____ _____.

신데렐라 이야기는 행복한 결말이 있다.

2 I was so _____ _____ see you there.

나는 너를 거기에서 만나서 너무 행복했다.

3 When we heard that news, we were _____ _____ _____.

우리는 그 소식을 듣고, 너에게 정말 잘된 일이라고 생각했다.

4 Spending time with my dog _____ _____ _____.

내 강아지와 시간을 보내는 것은 나를 행복하게 한다.

hard

1 I _____ _____ _____ _____ _____ no to people.

나는 사람들에게 안 된다고 거절하는 것을 잘 못했다.

2 It was _____ _____ _____ that he won the game.

그가 경기에서 이겼다는 것을 믿기 어려웠다.

3 The astronaut has a _____ _____ that requires teamwork.

우주 비행사는 팀워크가 필요한 힘든 일을 한다.

4 It was a _____ _____ for all of us.

그날은 우리 모두에게 힘든 날이었다.

> **Word Box** | astronaut 몡 우주 비행사 require 동 필요로 하다, 요구하다

Ⓐ **Expressions** 표현을 듣고, 큰 소리로 세 번씩 읽어 보세요.

MP3-103

heavy

[hévi] 혱 무거운, 많은, 심한

❶ heavy rain
큰 비, 폭우

❷ heavy traffic
심한 교통 체증

❸ heavy workload
과중한 업무량

❹ heavy schedule
빡빡한 일정

high

[hai] 혱 높은, 높이가 ~인

❶ high level
높은 수준

❷ high quality
고품질(의)

❸ high standard
높은 기준

❹ high expectations
높은 기대치

Ⓑ Check the Expressions

문장을 듣고, 빈칸에 알맞은 단어를 써 보세요.

heavy

1 _____ _____ caused flooding in the streets.

폭우로 도로에 홍수가 발생했다.

2 Manhattan is notorious for _____ _____.

맨해튼은 교통 체증으로 악명이 높다.

3 He suffered from a _____ _____.

그는 과중한 업무량으로 고통받았다.

4 I have a _____ _____ this week.

나는 이번 주 일정이 빠듯하다.

high

⭐ I'm getting ~~high~~. (X) 나는 키가 크고 있다. I'm getting tall. (O)

1 She showed us a _____ _____ of skill on the ice.

그녀는 빙판에서 높은 수준의 기술을 우리에게 선보였다.

2 You can get _____ _____ goods at low prices.

너는 고품질의 물건들을 저렴한 가격에 살 수 있다.

3 They set a _____ _____ for their products.

그들은 제품에 대해 높은 기준을 정했습니다.

4 My parents have _____ _____ for my future.

우리 부모님은 내 미래에 대해 높은 기대치를 가지고 계시다.

Word Box | workload 圐 작업량, 업무량 notorious 圐 악명 높은 suffer from ~로 고통받다

Unit 05 | Review the Expressions

A ⓐ와 ⓑ에서 알맞은 단어를 하나씩 골라 표현을 완성하고, 우리말 뜻을 써 보세요.

ⓐ	ⓑ
hard heavy high happy	ending job standard traffic

1 _____ _____ _____

2 _____ _____ _____

3 _____ _____ _____

4 _____ _____ _____

B 주어진 단어를 빈칸에 알맞게 배열하여 문장을 완성해 보세요.

1 I _____ meet new people.
   (happy / was / to)

2 I _____ understanding his directions.
   (a / hard / time / had)

3 I have _____ this month.
   (heavy / a / schedule)

4 She showed us _____ on the field.
   (a / level / of / skill / high)

C 문장의 빈칸에 우리말 뜻에 맞는 표현을 써 보세요.

1 When we heard that news, we were _____ _____ _____.
너를 위해 기쁜

2 It was _____ _____ _____ that he won the game.
믿기 어려운

3 _____ _____ caused flooding in the streets.
큰 비

4 You can get _____ _____ goods at low prices.
고품질의

D 다음 글의 빈칸에 알맞은 표현을 우리말 뜻을 보고 써 보세요.

1
> Yesterday was a _____ _____ for me. Everything seemed
> 힘든 날
>
> difficult, and I felt exhausted. However, a surprise visit from my best
>
> friend _____ _____ _____. His kind words cheered me
> 날 기쁘게 했다
>
> up.

2
> I have a _____ _____ at my new school. There are many
> 많은 공부량
>
> tasks to complete. My teachers have _____ _____ for
> 높은 기대치
>
> my performance. I'll do my best to meet them and prove myself
>
> capable.

Expression Check List

√	표현	√	표현
	bad habit		common language
	bad mood		common knowledge
	bad temper		common name
	go bad		common enemy
	big deal		deep sleep
	big disappointment		deep trouble
	big mistake		deep thought
	big surprise		deep breath
	bright color		direct flight
	bright future		direct quote
	bright idea		direct experience
	bright side		direct message
	chilly morning		early spring
	chilly air		early start
	chilly wind		early days
	chilly weather		early bird
	clear message		easy money
	clear understanding		easy question
	make something clear		easy to
	crystal clear		take it easy

√	표현	√	표현
	empty space		great success
	empty promise		great opportunity
	feel empty		great pride
	empty-handed		a great deal of
	excellent job		happy ending
	excellent grade		happy to
	excellent condition		happy for someone
	excellent choice		make someone happy
	full name		have a hard time ~ing
	full moon		hard to believe
	full-time		hard job
	full of energy		hard day
	front page		heavy rain
	front seat		heavy traffic
	front row		heavy workload
	in front of		heavy schedule
	good chance		high level
	good luck		high quality
	good enough		high standard
	good at		high expectations

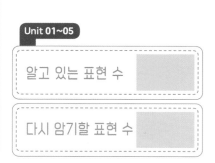

Unit 01~05

알고 있는 표현 수

다시 암기할 표현 수

Ⓐ Expressions 표현을 듣고, 큰 소리로 세 번씩 읽어 보세요.

MP3-105

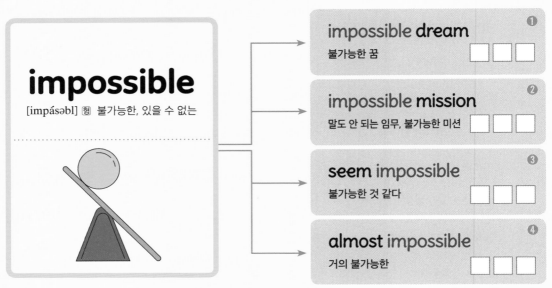

impossible

[impásəbl] 형 불가능한, 있을 수 없는

❶ **impossible dream**
불가능한 꿈

❷ **impossible mission**
말도 안 되는 임무, 불가능한 미션

❸ **seem impossible**
불가능한 것 같다

❹ **almost impossible**
거의 불가능한

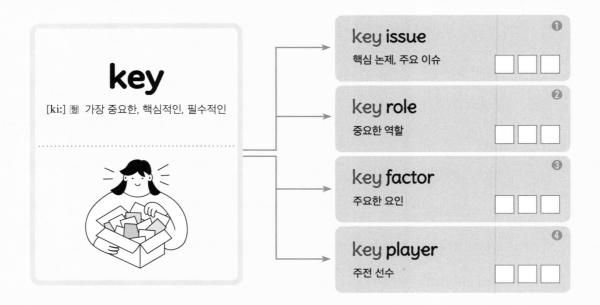

key

[ki:] 형 가장 중요한, 핵심적인, 필수적인

❶ **key issue**
핵심 논제, 주요 이슈

❷ **key role**
중요한 역할

❸ **key factor**
주요한 요인

❹ **key player**
주전 선수

Ⓑ Check the Expressions

문장을 듣고, 빈칸에 알맞은 단어를 써 보세요.

MP3-106

impossible   ★ It was a ~~very~~ impossible job. (X) impossible은 very와 함께 쓸 수 없음.

1 Traveling to outer space seemed like an _____ _____.

먼 우주로의 여행은 불가능한 꿈처럼 보였다.

2 The team was faced with an _____ _____.

그 팀은 말도 안 되는 임무를 맡게 되었다.

3 It _____ _____ that he could finish it today.

그가 오늘까지 그것을 끝내는 것은 불가능한 것 같다.

4 It's _____ _____ to imagine a world without music.

음악 없는 세상을 상상하는 것은 거의 불가능하다.

key

1 Global warming became the _____ _____.

지구 온난화는 핵심 논제가 되었다.

2 Education plays a _____ _____ in providing equal opportunities.

교육은 동등한 기회를 부여하는 데 핵심적인 역할을 한다.

3 Vocabulary is a _____ _____ in learning English.

어휘는 영어를 배우는 데 핵심 요소이다.

4 Julie is a _____ _____ in our soccer team.

줄리는 우리 축구팀의 주전 선수이다.

Word Box | factor 몡 요인, 요소 equal 혱 동일한, 평등한 vocabulary 몡 어휘, 용어

Ⓐ Expressions 표현을 듣고, 큰 소리로 세 번씩 읽어 보세요.

MP3-107

large

[la:rʤ] 형 큰, (양이) 많은, 광범위한

❶ a large **amount of**
많은 양의

❷ a large **number of**
많은 수의

❸ large **population**
많은 인구, 큰 집단

❹ large **proportion**
많은 비율

long

[lɔ:ŋ] 형 긴, 길이가 ~인, 힘든
부 오래, 오랫동안

❶ long **day**
힘든 하루, 긴 하루

❷ long **way**
먼 곳, 먼 길

❸ long **face**
시무룩한 얼굴

❹ **as** long **as**
~이기만 하면, ~하는 한

Ⓑ Check the Expressions

문장을 듣고, 빈칸에 알맞은 단어를 써 보세요.

large ⭐ A large amount of money ~~are~~ given. (X) A large amount of money is given. (O)

1 The storage was filled with _____ _____ _____ _____ goods.

그 창고는 많은 물건들로 가득 차 있었다.

2 The stationery store had _____ _____ _____ _____ pens.

그 문구점엔 많은 수의 펜이 있었다.

3 India is a country with a _____ _____.

인도는 인구가 많은 나라이다.

4 A _____ _____ of older people need care and support.

노인 인구의 상당 비율은 보살핌과 지원이 필요하다.

long

1 I spent a _____ _____ playing baseball with my friends.

나는 친구들과 야구를 하며 긴 하루를 보냈다.

2 They still have a _____ _____ to go.

그들은 아직 갈 길이 많이 남아 있다.

3 She had a _____ _____ when she made a mistake.

그녀는 실수했을 때 시무룩한 얼굴이 되었다.

4 I don't mind _____ _____ _____ it doesn't take too long.

너무 오래 걸리지만 않는다면 나는 상관없다.

Word Box | storage 명 저장고, 보관소, 저장 stationery 명 문구류, 문방구 mind 동 상관하다, 언짢아 하다

A ⓐ와 ⓑ에서 알맞은 단어를 하나씩 골라 표현을 완성하고, 우리말 뜻을 써 보세요.

ⓐ	ⓑ
long large impossible key	dream way proportion issue

1 _____ _____

2 _____ _____

3 _____ _____

4 _____ _____

B 주어진 단어를 빈칸에 알맞게 배열하여 문장을 완성해 보세요.

1 _____ that he could win the game.
  (It / impossible / seems)

2 Education _____ shaping our future.
  (plays / key / a / role / in)

3 The factory was filled with _____ goods.
  (a / amount / of / large)

4 I _____ practicing my presentation.
  (a / spent / long / day)

문장의 빈칸에 우리말 뜻에 맞는 표현을 써 보세요.

1 It's _____ _____ to imagine a world without music.
      거의 불가능한

2 Vocabulary is a _____ _____ in learning English.
                    핵심적인 요인

3 The stationery store had _____ _____ _____ _____ pens.
                                        많은 수의

4 I don't mind _____ _____ _____ it doesn't take too long.
                  ~하는 한

D 다음 글의 빈칸에 알맞은 표현을 우리말 뜻을 보고 써 보세요.

1
In a big city with a _____ _____, the brave heroes
                            많은 인구
accepted an _____ _____. They faced challenges and
                  불가능한 임무
brought hope to the people. Their courage showed that anything is
possible.

2
Boram was a _____ _____ in the final match. She felt
                  주전 선수
nervous and had a _____ _____ because she made a
                        시무룩한 얼굴
mistake. However, her teacher reminded her that mistakes happen.
With the encouragement, she regained confidence.

Unit 07 natural / new / personal / quick

Ⓐ Expressions 표현을 듣고, 큰 소리로 세 번씩 읽어 보세요.

MP3-109

natural
[nǽtʃrəl] 혱 자연의, 자연 발생적인, 정상적인

❶ **natural** cause 자연적인 원인	☐☐☐
❷ **natural** resource 천연자원	☐☐☐
❸ **natural** disaster 천재지변, 자연재해	☐☐☐
❹ **natural** history 자연사, 박물학	☐☐☐

new
[nu:] 혱 새, 새로운

❶ **new** generation 새로운 세대	☐☐☐
❷ **new** to someone ~에게 새로운	☐☐☐
❸ **new** record 신기록	☐☐☐
❹ brand **new** 신상품인, 완전히 새로운	☐☐☐

Ⓑ Check the Expressions

문장을 듣고, 빈칸에 알맞은 단어를 써 보세요.

natural

1 The forest fire was started by a _____ _____.

산불은 자연적인 원인으로 발생했다.

2 Solar energy and wind power are renewable _____ _____.

태양 에너지와 풍력은 재생 가능한 천연자원들이다.

3 It was one of the worst _____ _____ in history.

그것은 역사상 최악의 자연재해 중 하나였다.

4 I've visited the _____ _____ Museum in Washington D.C.

나는 워싱턴 디시에 있는 자연사 박물관을 방문했다.

new   ★ I bought a ~~blue new~~ notebook. (X) I bought a new blue notebook. (O)

1 The _____ _____ of electric cars can be charged faster.

차세대 전기차는 충전이 더 빨리 될 수 있다.

2 Indian food was completely _____ _____ _____.

인도 음식은 나에게 완전히 새로웠다.

3 Their latest album set a _____ _____.

그들의 최신 앨범은 신기록을 세웠다.

4 Our family bought a _____ _____ car.

우리 가족은 최신형 자동차를 샀다.

Word Box | generation 몡 세대 renewable 혱 재생 가능한 charge 툉 충전하다

MP3-111

Ⓐ **Expressions**   표현을 듣고, 큰 소리로 세 번씩 읽어 보세요.

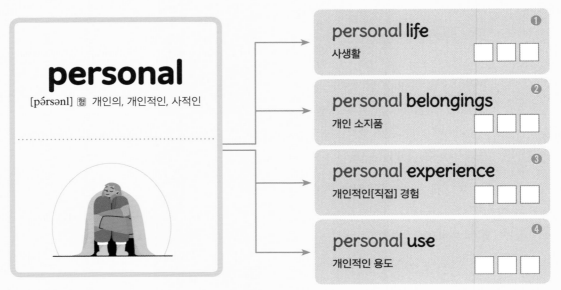

personal

[pə́rsənl] 형 개인의, 개인적인, 사적인

❶ personal life
사생활

❷ personal belongings
개인 소지품

❸ personal experience
개인적인[직접] 경험

❹ personal use
개인적인 용도

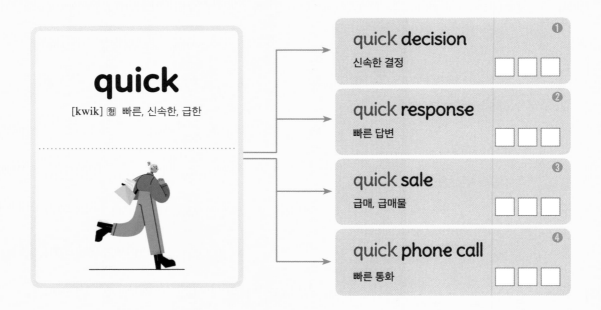

quick

[kwik] 형 빠른, 신속한, 급한

❶ quick decision
신속한 결정

❷ quick response
빠른 답변

❸ quick sale
급매, 급매물

❹ quick phone call
빠른 통화

Ⓑ Check the Expressions

문장을 듣고, 빈칸에 알맞은 단어를 써 보세요.

MP3-112

personal

⭐ personal 혱 vs. personnel 몡 어떤 조직의 인원

1 He doesn't answer questions about his _____ _____.

그는 개인 사생활에 관한 질문에는 대답하지 않는다.

2 Don't forget to bring _____ _____ with you.

개인 소지품 챙기는 것을 잊지 마세요.

3 We shared our _____ _____ in the history class.

우리는 역사 시간에 개인적인 경험들에 대해 이야기를 나누었다.

4 She bought a new laptop for _____ _____.

그녀는 개인적인 용도로 새 노트북을 샀다.

quick

1 People asked him to make a _____ _____.

사람들은 그에게 빠른 결정을 요구했다.

2 She sent a _____ _____ to my email.

그녀는 나의 이메일에 빠른 답변을 보내 주었다.

3 I looked at the flea market for a _____ _____.

나는 빠른 판매를 위해 벼룩시장을 알아보았다.

4 Can I make one _____ _____ _____?

급하게 전화 한 통 해도 될까요?

> **Word Box** | belongings 몡 재산, 소유물 flea market 몡 벼룩시장

A   ⓐ와 ⓑ에서 알맞은 단어를 하나씩 골라 표현을 완성하고, 우리말 뜻을 써 보세요.

ⓐ	ⓑ
natural personal new quick	experience record history response

1   _____   _____

2   _____   _____

3   _____   _____

4   _____   _____

B   주어진 단어를 빈칸에 알맞게 배열하여 문장을 완성해 보세요.

1   It could be one of _____.
      (the / disasters / worst / natural)

2   Mexican food was _____.
      (completely / to / me / new)

3   I prefer not to answer questions _____.
      (my / about / life / personal)

4   They asked him to _____.
      (decision / make / a / quick)

C 문장의 빈칸에 우리말 뜻에 맞는 표현을 써 보세요.

1 The forest fire was started by a _____ _____.

자연적인 원인

2 Our family bought a _____ _____ car.

신상의, 완전히 새 것인

3 Don't forget to bring _____ _____ with you.

개인적인 소지품

4 Can I make one _____ _____ _____?

빠른 전화 통화

D 다음 글의 빈칸에 알맞은 표현을 우리말 뜻을 보고 써 보세요.

1
> In the world, we have _____ _____ like
> 천연자원들
> water, air and trees. They are important for survival. The
> _____ _____ must learn to protect and conserve these
> 새로운 세대
> resources for a better future.

2
> When we have something we no longer need, we can sell it.
> A _____ _____ means we can sell it fast. We can use the
> 급매
> money for our _____ _____ or save it for something
> 개인적인 용도
> special.

Unit 08
rich / serious / severe / steady

Ⓐ **Expressions** 표현을 듣고, 큰 소리로 세 번씩 읽어 보세요.

 MP3-113

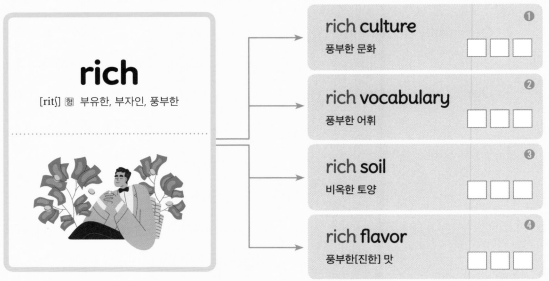

rich

[ritʃ] 형 부유한, 부자인, 풍부한

❶ rich **culture**
풍부한 문화

❷ rich **vocabulary**
풍부한 어휘

❸ rich **soil**
비옥한 토양

❹ rich **flavor**
풍부한[진한] 맛

serious

[síriəs] 형 심각한, 진지한, 중대한

❶ serious **illness**
중병

❷ serious **problem**
중대한 문제

❸ serious **crime**
중범죄

❹ serious **threat**
심각한 위협

Ⓑ Check the Expressions

문장을 듣고, 빈칸에 알맞은 단어를 써 보세요.

rich

1 The city has a _____ _____ and a diverse population.

그 도시는 풍부한 문화와 다양한 인구 구성을 가지고 있다.

2 Reading books helps students develop a _____ _____.

독서는 학생들이 풍부한 어휘력을 키우는 데 도움을 준다.

3 Trees and flowers grow best in _____ _____.

나무와 꽃들은 비옥한 토양에서 가장 잘 자란다.

4 The cake is soft and has a _____ _____.

그 케이크는 부드럽고 맛이 풍부하다.

serious   ⭐ She has serious headache. (X) She had a serious headache. (O)

1 He has just overcome a _____ _____.

그는 막 중병을 이겨냈다.

2 The country is facing a _____ economic _____.

그 나라는 중대한 경제 문제에 직면해 있다.

3 The police are investigating a _____ _____.

경찰들은 중범죄를 수사중이다.

4 Climate change is a _____ _____ to our planet.

기후 변화는 지구에 심각한 위협이다.

Word Box | diverse 휑 다양한 overcome 동 극복하다 investigate 동 수사하다 climate 명 기후

Ⓐ Expressions 표현을 듣고, 큰 소리로 세 번씩 읽어 보세요.

MP3-115

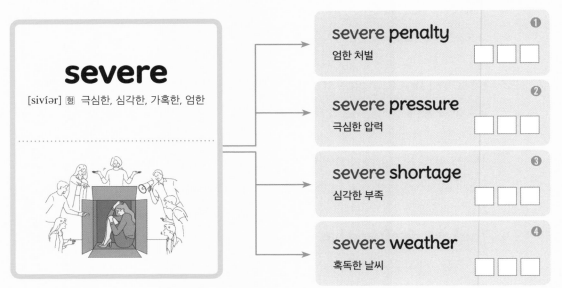

severe
[sivíər] 형 극심한, 심각한, 가혹한, 엄한

❶ severe penalty
엄한 처벌

❷ severe pressure
극심한 압력

❸ severe shortage
심각한 부족

❹ severe weather
혹독한 날씨

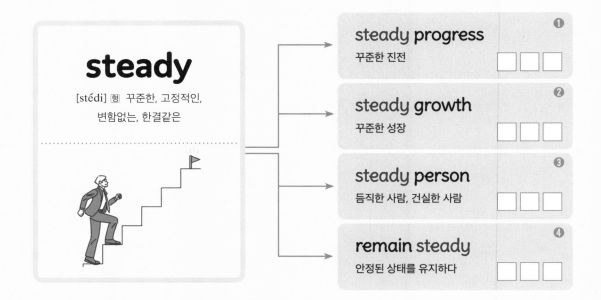

steady
[stédi] 형 꾸준한, 고정적인,
변함없는, 한결같은

❶ steady progress
꾸준한 진전

❷ steady growth
꾸준한 성장

❸ steady person
듬직한 사람, 건실한 사람

❹ remain steady
안정된 상태를 유지하다

Ⓑ Check the Expressions

문장을 듣고, 빈칸에 알맞은 단어를 써 보세요.

MP3-116

severe

1 The terrorist was sentenced to a _____ _____.

그 테러리스트는 중형을 선고받았다.

2 I was under _____ _____ to succeed in my exams.

나는 시험을 잘 봐야 한다는 극심한 압력을 받았다.

3 There is a _____ _____ of clean water in the world.

세계적으로 깨끗한 물이 심각하게 부족하다.

4 Emperor penguins can live in _____ _____.

황제펭귄은 혹독한 날씨에도 살 수 있다.

steady

★ She worked ~~steady~~ all day. (X) She worked steadily all day. (O)

1 The scientist made _____ _____ in his research.

그 과학자는 자기 연구에서 꾸준한 진전을 이루었다.

2 The population has shown _____ _____ for the past five years.

인구는 지난 5년간 꾸준한 성장세를 보여줬다.

3 He is a _____ _____ who is always there for me.

그는 항상 나를 위해 그곳에 있어주는 듬직한 사람이다.

4 The weather _____ _____ throughout the day.

날씨는 하루 종일 안정적이었다.

Word Box | be sentenced to (형을) 선고받다 throughout 전 ~동안 쭉, 내내

A ⓐ와 ⓑ에서 알맞은 단어를 하나씩 골라 표현을 완성하고, 우리말 뜻을 써 보세요.

ⓐ	ⓑ
rich serious steady severe	vocabulary growth penalty threat

1 [   ] _____

2 [   ] _____

3 [   ] _____

4 [   ] _____

B 주어진 단어를 빈칸에 알맞게 배열하여 문장을 완성해 보세요.

1 The country _____ and a diverse population.
(rich / has / a / culture)

2 Linda has just overcome _____.
(a / illness / serious)

3 He was _____ to meet the deadline for the project.
(severe / under / pressure)

4 _____ throughout the weekend.
(The weather / steady / remained)

C 문장의 빈칸에 우리말 뜻에 맞는 표현을 써 보세요.

1 The cake is soft and has a _____ _____.
풍부한 맛, 진한 맛

2 The police are investigating a _____ _____.
중범죄

3 There is a _____ _____ of clean water in the world.
심각한 부족

4 He is a _____ _____ who is always there for me.
듬직한 사람

D 다음 글의 빈칸에 알맞은 표현을 우리말 뜻을 보고 써 보세요.

1
_____ _____ is essential for growing healthy plants.
비옥한 토양
Therefore, soil pollution is a _____ _____ that can harm
심각한 문제
plants. Farmers can help protect their soil from pollution by avoid-
ing the use of harmful chemicals.

2
Kara was under _____ _____ to win the race, but she
극심한 부담감
maintained _____ _____ throughout the competition.
지속적인 발전
She started off slowly, but she gradually picked up speed.

Ⓐ Expressions 표현을 듣고, 큰 소리로 세 번씩 읽어 보세요.

MP3-117

strong

[strɔːŋ] 형 강한, 힘센, 강력한,
~을 잘하는, 권력 있는

❶ **strong desire**
강렬한 소망, 열망
☐ ☐ ☐

❷ **strong influence**
강력한 영향
☐ ☐ ☐

❸ **strong supporter**
확고한 지지자
☐ ☐ ☐

❹ **strong opponent**
강적, 버거운 상대
☐ ☐ ☐

terrible

[térəbl] 형 끔찍한, 심한, 좋지 않은

❶ **terrible accident**
끔찍한 사고
☐ ☐ ☐

❷ **in terrible pain**
심한 고통을 느끼는
☐ ☐ ☐

❸ **terrible mess**
엉망진창
☐ ☐ ☐

❹ **terrible outcome**
최악의 결과(물)
☐ ☐ ☐

ⒷCheck the Expressions

문장을 듣고, 빈칸에 알맞은 단어를 써 보세요.

MP3-118

strong

⭐ He has strong opinion. (X) He has a strong opinion. (O)

1 She had a _____ _____ for success.

그녀는 성공에 대한 열망을 가지고 있었다.

2 My parents had a _____ _____ on my values.

우리 부모님은 나의 가치관에 강한 영향을 주셨다.

3 He is a _____ _____ of his favorite sports team.

그는 자기가 좋아하는 스포츠 팀의 강력한 지지자이다.

4 They are _____ _____ of animal testing.

그들은 동물 실험을 강력히 반대하는 사람들이다.

terrible

1 The _____ _____ caused traffic congestion.

끔찍한 사건으로 교통체증이 발생했다.

2 The patient was _____ _____ _____ after the surgery.

그 환자는 수술 후에 엄청난 고통을 느꼈다.

3 The kitchen was a _____ _____ after the party.

파티가 끝난 후 부엌은 엉망진창이 되었다.

4 The _____ _____ of the war was the loss of millions of lives.

전쟁의 끔찍한 결과는 수백만 명의 인명 손실이었다.

Word Box | opponent 몡 상대, 반대자 congestion 몡 혼잡, 체증 surgery 몡 수술 loss 몡 손실

Ⓐ Expressions 표현을 듣고, 큰 소리로 세 번씩 읽어 보세요.

MP3-119

true
[tru:] 형 사실인, 참인, 맞는, 진짜의

❶ true story
실화 ☐☐☐

❷ true love
진정한 사랑 ☐☐☐

❸ one's true identity
~의 진짜 신분[정체] ☐☐☐

❹ true value
진정한 가치 ☐☐☐

valuable
[vǽljuəbl] 형 소중한, 귀중한,
가치가 큰, 값비싼

❶ valuable lesson
값진 교훈 ☐☐☐

❷ valuable information
값진 정보 ☐☐☐

❸ valuable asset
귀중한 자산 ☐☐☐

❹ valuable time
소중한 시간 ☐☐☐

ⓑ Check the Expressions

문장을 듣고, 빈칸에 알맞은 단어를 써 보세요.

true

1 I read a _____ _____ about a dog which rescued people.

나는 사람들을 구한 개에 관한 실화를 읽었다.

2 I don't know what the _____ _____ is.

나는 진정한 사랑이 무엇인지 모르겠다.

3 The alien finally revealed _____ _____ _____.

그 외계인은 마침내 그것의 진짜 정체를 드러냈다.

4 The _____ _____ of friendship is more than just playing together.

우정의 진정한 가치는 함께 노는 것 그 이상이다.

valuable

1 I learned a _____ _____ from my mistakes.

나는 실수를 통해 값진 교훈을 배웠다.

2 We found some _____ _____ on the internet.

우리는 인터넷에서 값진 정보를 발견했다.

3 Students with a positive attitude are _____ _____.

긍정적인 태도를 가진 학생들은 값진 자산이다.

4 Use your _____ _____ wisely by planning ahead.

미리 계획을 세워서 당신의 귀중한 시간을 현명하게 사용하세요.

Word Box | identity 몡 정체, 신분 asset 몡 자산, 재산 rescue 통 구하다, 구조하다 reveal 통 드러내다

A ⓐ와 ⓑ에서 알맞은 단어를 하나씩 골라 표현을 완성하고, 우리말 뜻을 써 보세요.

ⓐ	ⓑ
strong terrible true valuable	supporter time outcome story

1 _____   _____

2 _____   _____

3 _____   _____

4 _____   _____

B 주어진 단어를 빈칸에 알맞게 배열하여 문장을 완성해 보세요.

1 My parents _____ on my values.
(had / influence / a / strong)

2 The patient _____ after the surgery.
(in / was / terrible / pain)

3 The _____ is priceless.
(value / true / of / friendship)

4 I _____ from my experience.
(valuable / learned / a / lesson)

C 문장의 빈칸에 우리말 뜻에 맞는 표현을 써 보세요.

1 They are _____ _____ of animal testing.
강력한 반대자들

2 The kitchen was a _____ _____ after the party.
엉망진창

3 The alien finally revealed its _____ _____.
진짜 정체

4 We found some _____ _____ on the internet.
값진 정보

D 다음 글의 빈칸에 알맞은 표현을 우리말 뜻을 보고 써 보세요.

1

A little bird, Sammy, had a _____ _____ and hurt his
끔찍한 사고

wings. But he had a _____ _____ to fly. Sammy never gave
강한 소망

up. He practiced and believed. One day, his dream came true, and

he soared high. He inspired others with his positive attitude.

2

After the accident, I discovered the power of _____ _____.
진정한 사랑

I understood that love brought joy and happiness. I realized that

family and friends were the most _____ _____ in my life.
소중한 자산들

Expression Check List

➡ 아는 표현 앞에 √ 표시를 해 보세요. 기억나지 않는 표현은 다시 확인해 암기하세요.

√	표현	√	표현
	impossible dream		new generation
	impossible mission		new to someone
	seem impossible		new record
	almost impossible		brand new
	key issue		personal life
	key role		personal belongings
	key factor		personal experience
	key player		personal use
	a large amount of		quick decision
	a large number of		quick response
	large population		quick sale
	large proportion		quick phone call
	long day		rich culture
	long way		rich vocabulary
	long face		rich soil
	as long as		rich flavor
	natural cause		serious illness
	natural resource		serious problem
	natural disaster		serious crime
	natural history		serious threat

√	표현	√	표현
	severe penalty		valuable lesson
	severe pressure		valuable information
	severe shortage		valuable asset
	severe weather		valuable time
	steady progress		
	steady growth		
	steady person		
	remain steady		
	strong desire		
	strong influence		
	strong supporter		
	strong opponent		
	terrible accident		
	in terrible pain		
	terrible mess		
	terrible outcome		
	true story		
	true love		
	one's true identity		
	true value		

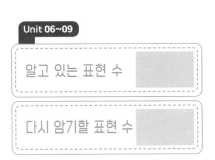

Unit 06~09

알고 있는 표현 수

다시 암기할 표현 수

Chapter 4

부사와
영어표현

absolutely / deeply / strongly / fully

Ⓐ **Expressions** 표현을 듣고, 큰 소리로 세 번씩 읽어 보세요.

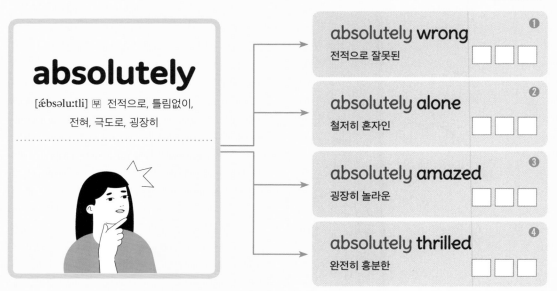

absolutely

[ǽbsəluːtli] 뜀 전적으로, 틀림없이, 전혀, 극도로, 굉장히

❶ absolutely **wrong**
전적으로 잘못된

❷ absolutely **alone**
철저히 혼자인

❸ absolutely **amazed**
굉장히 놀라운

❹ absolutely **thrilled**
완전히 흥분한

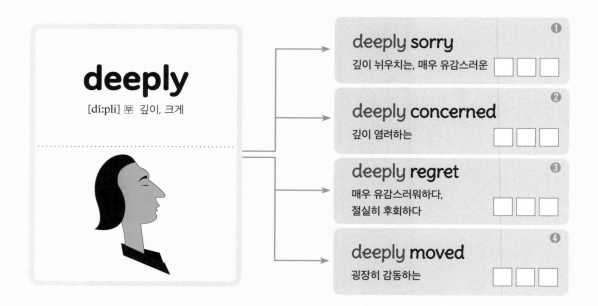

deeply

[díːpli] 뜀 깊이, 크게

❶ deeply **sorry**
깊이 뉘우치는, 매우 유감스러운

❷ deeply **concerned**
깊이 염려하는

❸ deeply **regret**
매우 유감스러워하다,
절실히 후회하다

❹ deeply **moved**
굉장히 감동하는

ⒷCheck the Expressions

문장을 듣고, 빈칸에 알맞은 단어를 써 보세요.

absolutely

1 He was _____ _____ about his answer.

그는 답변이 완전히 틀렸다.

2 Kevin was _____ _____ in the house.

케빈은 집에 완전히 혼자 있었다.

⭐ I was ~~absolute~~ alone. (X)

3 I was _____ _____ by the beauty of Jeju Island.

나는 제주도의 아름다움에 매우 놀랐다.

4 They were _____ _____ to win the election.

그들은 선거에 이겨서 완전히 흥분했다.

deeply

1 I am _____ _____ for what I said.

나는 내가 말한 것에 대해 깊이 뉘우친다.

2 They are _____ _____ about the terrorist attack.

그들은 테러리스트들의 공격에 깊이 염려한다.

3 He has _____ _____ not working hard on his test.

그는 시험 공부를 열심히 하지 않은 것을 뼈저리게 후회했다.

4 We were _____ _____ by the performance of the actors.

우리는 배우들의 연기에 깊이 감동받았다.

Word Box | thrilled 형 아주 흥분한, 황홀해 하는 performance 명 공연, 연기

Unit 01 · absolutely / deeply / strongly / fully

Ⓐ Expressions
표현을 듣고, 큰 소리로 세 번씩 읽어 보세요.

MP3-123

strongly

[strɔ́:ŋli] 분 강하게, 완강히, 튼튼하게, 열심히

❶ strongly **disagree**
절대 반대하다[동의하지 않다] □□□

❷ strongly **suggest**
강력하게 제안하다 □□□

❸ strongly **recommend**
강하게 추천하다 □□□

❹ strongly **criticize**
맹렬히 비난하다 □□□

fully

[fúli] 분 완전히, 전적으로, 충분히

❶ fully **aware**
충분히 인식하는 □□□

❷ fully **awake**
완전히 깨어 있는 □□□

❸ fully **appreciate**
진가를 완전히 알아주다, 충분히 인정하다 □□□

❹ fully **recover**
(건강이) 완전히 회복하다 □□□

Ⓑ Check the Expressions

문장을 듣고, 빈칸에 알맞은 단어를 써 보세요.

MP3-124

strongly

1 I _____ _____ with your decision.

나는 당신의 결정에 전혀 동의하지 않습니다.

2 I _____ _____ that you take a break from work.

일을 조금 쉬는 것을 나는 강력히 권고합니다.

3 I _____ _____ that you watch the movie *Avatar*.

나는 너에게 영화 <아바타>를 보라고 강력히 추천한다.

4 The artist was _____ _____ for his latest work.

그 예술가는 그의 최근 작품에 대해 강한 비판을 받았다.

fully

⭐ I ~~fully don't understand~~ what he's saying. (X)
I don't fully understand what he's saying. (O)

1 The driver was _____ _____ of the speed limit.

그 운전자는 속도 제한을 충분히 인지했다.

2 The soldier was _____ _____ during the night watch.

그 군인은 불침번을 서는 중에 완전히 깨어 있었다.

3 I _____ _____ your help and support.

나는 당신의 도움과 지원을 진심으로 감사히 생각합니다.

4 It took him months to _____ _____ from his injury.

그는 부상에서 완전히 회복되는 데 수개월이 걸렸다.

Word Box | criticize 동 비판하다, 비난하다 latest 형 가장 최근의, 최신의 watch 명 망보기, 불침번

A 우리말 뜻에 맞게 빈칸에 알맞은 단어를 써 보세요.

1 전적으로 잘못된   _____   <u>wrong</u>

2 절실히 후회하다   <u>deeply</u>   _____

3 맹렬히 비난하다   _____   _____

4 완전히 회복하다   _____   _____

B ⓐ와 ⓑ에서 단어 하나씩을 골라 써 문장을 완성하세요.

ⓐ	ⓑ
absolutely fully strongly deeply	amazed recommend concerned awake

1 I was _____ by the beauty of Jeju island.

2 They are _____ about the terrorist attack.

3 I _____ that you watch the movie *Avatar*.

4 The soldier was _____ during the night watch.

C 문장의 빈칸에 우리말 뜻에 맞는 표현을 써 보세요.

1 They were _____ _____ to win the election.
완전히 흥분한

2 We were _____ _____ by the performance of the actors.
깊이 감동받은

3 I _____ _____ that you take a break from work.
강력하게 제안하다

4 I _____ _____ your help and support.
매우 고맙게 생각하다

D 다음 대화의 빈칸에 알맞은 표현을 우리말 뜻을 보고 써 보세요.

A I can't believe I was left _____ _____ in that spooky house!
철저히 혼자인

B Oh no, that must have been frightening. I'm _____ _____
매우 유감스러운

you had to go through that.

A It was a terrible experience, but I'm glad it's over now.

B I _____ _____ with leaving someone alone in such a
절대 반대하다

situation.

A I appreciate your support. I was _____ _____ of the risks,
충분히 인식하는

but it was still challenging.

Common adverb collocations

Ⓐ Expressions 표현을 듣고, 큰 소리로 세 번씩 읽어 보세요.

MP3-125

❶ actively [ǽktivli]
㊾ 적극적으로

actively involved
적극적으로 관여하는
☐ ☐ ☐

❷ badly [bǽdli]
㊾ 나쁘게, 심하게, 매우

badly hurt
심하게 다치다
☐ ☐ ☐

❸ bitterly [bítərli]
㊾ 비통하게, 몹시

bitterly cold
몹시 추운
☐ ☐ ☐

❹ closely [klóusli]
㊾ 밀접하게, 면밀히, 주의하여

closely examine
면밀히 검토하다
☐ ☐ ☐

❺ completely [kəmplíːtli]
㊾ 완전히, 전적으로

completely forget
완전히 잊다
☐ ☐ ☐

❻ firmly [fə́ːrmli]
㊾ 단호히, 확고히

firmly believe
굳게 믿다
☐ ☐ ☐

❼ greatly [gréitli]
㊾ 대단히, 크게

greatly admire
매우 동경[존경]하다
☐ ☐ ☐

❽ happily [hǽpili]
㊾ 행복하게, 운 좋게

happily married
행복하게 결혼 생활을 하고 있는
☐ ☐ ☐

Ⓑ Check the Expressions

문장을 듣고, 빈칸에 알맞은 단어를 써 보세요.

1 John's parents are _____ _____ in his education.

존의 부모님은 그의 교육에 적극적으로 관여하신다.

2 Tom fell off his bike and was _____ _____.

톰은 자전거에서 떨어져서 크게 다쳤다.

3 The animals sought shelter from the _____ _____ weather.

동물들은 몹시 추운 날씨를 피할 피난처를 찾았다.

4 The detective _____ _____ the crime scene for clues.

그 형사는 단서들을 찾기 위해 범죄 현장을 면밀히 조사했다.

5 He _____ _____ his lines in the school play.

그는 학교 연극에서 자신의 대사를 완전히 잊어버렸다.

6 I _____ _____ in the importance of teamwork.

나는 팀워크의 중요성을 굳게 믿는다.

7 They _____ _____ the famous singers for their success.

그들은 유명 가수들의 성공을 크게 동경한다.

8 They have been _____ _____ for over 50 years.

그들은 50년 넘게 행복한 결혼 생활을 해왔다.

Word Box | seek 图 찾다, 추구하다(과거형 sought) scene 명 현장, 장면 clue 명 단서, 실마리 line 명 선, 줄, 대사, 가사

Common adverb collocations

Ⓐ **Expressions** 표현을 듣고, 큰 소리로 세 번씩 읽어 보세요.

MP3-127

❶ highly [háili]
🄫 대단히, 매우

highly intelligent
대단히 총명한, 지능이 높은
☐ ☐ ☐

❷ perfectly [pə́ːrfiktli]
🄫 완전히, 지극히

perfectly normal
완벽하게 정상인
☐ ☐ ☐

❸ pretty [príti]
🄫 매우, 꽤

pretty good
매우 좋은
☐ ☐ ☐

❹ quite [kwait]
🄫 꽤, 상당히, 완전히

quite sure
꽤 확실한
☐ ☐ ☐

❺ seriously [síəriəsli]
🄫 심각하게, 진심으로

seriously doubt
심각하게 의심하다
☐ ☐ ☐

❻ slightly [sláitli]
🄫 약간, 조금

slightly different
살짝 다른
☐ ☐ ☐

❼ totally [tóutəli]
🄫 완전히, 전적으로

totally agree
완전히 동의하다
☐ ☐ ☐

❽ widely [wáidli]
🄫 널리, 폭넓게

widely known
널리 알려진
☐ ☐ ☐

Ⓑ Check the Expressions

문장을 듣고, 빈칸에 알맞은 단어를 써 보세요.

1 The AI (Artificial Intelligence) system is _____ _____.

인공지능 시스템은 상당히 지능이 높다.

2 It's _____ _____ to feel nervous before a big presentation.

큰 발표 전에 긴장하는 것은 지극히 정상이다.

3 The weather is _____ _____ with a gentle breeze.

날씨는 바람이 솔솔 불어 매우 좋다.

4 I'm _____ _____ that he is innocent.

나는 그가 결백하다는 것을 매우 확신한다.

5 I _____ _____ the quality of that product.

나는 그 제품의 품질을 매우 의심한다.

6 Her idea is _____ _____ from mine.

그녀의 생각은 나와 살짝 다르다.

7 I _____ _____ with your suggestion.

나는 너의 제안에 완전히 동의한다.

8 Coca-Cola is a _____ _____ brand of soft drinks.

코카콜라는 청량음료의 브랜드로 널리 알려져 있다.

Word Box | gentle 형 온화한, 가벼운 breeze 명 산들바람 innocent 형 무죄인, 결백한

A 우리말 뜻에 맞게 빈칸에 알맞은 단어를 써 보세요.

1 매우 동경[존경]하다 _____ _____

2 행복한 결혼 생활을 하고 있는 _____ _____

3 완벽하게 정상인 _____ _____

4 완전히 동의하다 _____ _____

B ⓐ와 ⓑ에서 단어 하나씩을 골라 써 문장을 완성하세요.

ⓐ	ⓑ
completely bitterly widely highly	cold known forgot intelligent

1 The animals sought shelter from the _____ weather.

2 He _____ his lines in the school play.

3 The AI (Artificial Intelligence) system is _____.

4 Coca-Cola is a _____ brand of soft drinks.

C 문장의 빈칸에 우리말 뜻에 맞는 표현을 써 보세요.

1 John's parents are _____ _____ in his education.
적극적으로 관여하는

2 I _____ _____ in the importance of teamwork.
굳게 믿다

3 The weather is _____ _____ with a gentle breeze.
꽤 좋은

4 Her idea is _____ _____ from mine.
살짝 다른

D 다음 대화의 빈칸에 알맞은 표현을 우리말 뜻을 보고 써 보세요.

A I heard you fell off the bike. Are you okay?

B I'm _____ _____. The doctors need to _____ _____
심하게 다친   정밀하게 진찰하다
(면밀히 검토하다)

my injuries.

A I'm so sorry to hear that. Do you think you'll be able to return to
school soon?

B I _____ _____ it. It will take time to heal, but I'm
심각하게 의심하다

_____ _____ I'll be okay.
꽤 확실한

A I hope you get better soon.

Expression Check List

➡ 아는 표현 앞에 √ 표시를 해 보세요. 기억나지 않는 표현은 다시 확인해 암기하세요.

√	표현	√	표현
	absolutely wrong		completely forget
	absolutely alone		firmly believe
	absolutely amazed		greatly admire
	absolutely thrilled		happily married
	deeply sorry		highly intelligent
	deeply concerned		perfectly normal
	deeply regret		pretty good
	deeply moved		quite sure
	strongly disagree		seriously doubt
	strongly suggest		slightly different
	strongly recommend		totally agree
	strongly criticize		widely known
	fully aware		
	fully awake		
	fully appreciate		
	fully recover		
	actively involved		
	badly hurt		
	bitterly cold		
	closely examine		

Unit 01~02

알고 있는 표현 수 [ ]

다시 암기할 표현 수 [ ]

정답
풀이

Chapter 1 최다빈출동사와 영어표현

Unit 01 have / take

Check the Expressions ···················· p.13

1 had a, chat
2 had a fight
3 has a headache
4 had a nightmare
5 had an argument
6 has a, effect on
7 had an experience
8 have an opportunity

Check the Expressions ···················· p.15

1 take a class
2 take an exam
3 take advantage of
4 take a taxi
5 taking notes
6 Taking a risk
7 took part in
8 take place

Review the Expressions ···················· pp.16~17

A 1 had
2 take

B 1 have, argument
2 have, effect on
3 take advantage of
4 take, risk

C 1 O
2 X (have an opportunity)
3 X (took a part)
4 X (take a class)

D 1 had a fight
2 has a headache
3 take a taxi
4 take notes

Unit 02 do / make

Check the Expressions ···················· p.19

1 do your best
2 do your homework
3 do a good job
4 done something wrong
5 do their duty
6 do my chores
7 do exercise
8 do the dishes

Check the Expressions ···················· p.21

1 make a point
2 makes a speech
3 made a promise
4 make, mistake
5 made, progress
6 make up your mind
7 make a difference
8 make a mess

Review the Expressions ···················· pp.22~23

A 1 do
2 make

B 1 do something wrong
2 do, duty
3 make, mistake
4 make progress

C 1 O
2 X (do the dishes)
3 O
4 X (make a mess)

D 1 do, homework
2 do exercise
3 make a speech
4 made a promise

Unit 03 break / catch

Check the Expressions ···················· p.25

1 broke into pieces
2 break a law
3 broke my heart
4 broke a record
5 broke down
6 broke out
7 broke the spell
8 break the news to

Check the Expressions ···················· p.27

1 catch a ball
2 caught my eye
3 catch up with
4 catch a cold
5 caught fire
6 catch, attention
7 catch your breath
8 catch you later

Review the Expressions ···················· pp.28~29

A 1 broke
2 catch

B 1 break, heart
2 break, spell
3 catch up
4 catch, cold

C 1 O
2 O
3 O
4 X (caught ⇨ catch)

D 1 broke into pieces
2 break, law
3 catch, ball
4 caught fire

Unit 04　come / go

Check the Expressions ⋯⋯⋯⋯⋯ p.31

1 came from
2 come to an end
3 come up with
4 came to a conclusion
5 came, close
6 come along
7 came across
8 Come to think of it

Check the Expressions ⋯⋯⋯⋯⋯ p.33

1 go abroad
2 went shopping
3 went on a picnic
4 go ahead
5 go bankrupt
6 go online
7 go crazy
8 go over

Review the Expressions ⋯⋯⋯⋯⋯ pp.34~35

A 1 come
2 go
B 1 come from
2 come close
3 go crazy
4 go over
C 1 X (came to a conclusion)
2 X (come up with)
3 O
4 X (go to bankrupt)
D 1 come to, end
2 Come to think of it
3 went shopping
4 go online

Unit 05　get / keep

Check the Expressions ⋯⋯⋯⋯⋯ p.37

1 get a chance
2 got a clue
3 got fired
4 got tired of
5 get together
6 get dressed
7 get pregnant
8 got hurt

Check the Expressions ⋯⋯⋯⋯⋯ p.39

1 keep quiet
2 Keeping a diary
3 keep a secret
4 keep calm
5 keep in touch
6 keep up with
7 keep an eye on
8 Keep your distance

Review the Expressions ⋯⋯⋯⋯⋯ pp.40~41

A 1 get
2 keep
B 1 get dressed
2 get pregnant
3 keep, secret
4 keep up with
C 1 O
2 O
3 X (keep in touch)
4 O
D 1 get together
2 get hurt
3 keep quiet
4 kept a diary

Unit 06　give / save

Check the Expressions ⋯⋯⋯⋯⋯ p.43

1 give up
2 give an example
3 give an opinion
4 gave me directions
5 gave permission
6 gave, a, impression
7 give away
8 give me a break

Check the Expressions ⋯⋯⋯⋯⋯ p.45

1 save time
2 save energy
3 saved my life
4 save space
5 saved, money
6 saves a seat
7 save a file
8 save you, trouble

Review the Expressions ⋯⋯⋯⋯⋯ pp.46~47

A 1 give
2 save
B 1 give, impression
2 give, break
3 save energy
4 save, file
C 1 X (give an example)
2 O
3 X (saves a seat)
4 X (saved my life)
D 1 gave me directions
2 gave permission
3 save time
4 save money

Unit 01 arrive / answer / ask / believe

Check the Expressions p.53

arrive

1 arrive home
2 arrived on time
3 arrive shortly
4 arrived late

answer

1 answering the question
2 answer the phone
3 give you an answer
4 waiting for an answer

Check the Expressions p.55

ask

1 ask a favor
2 asked for advice
3 asked if
4 asked permission

believe

1 It's hard to believe that
2 Believe it or not
3 It is believed that
4 believe in

Review the Expressions .... pp.56~57

A 1 on time
2 an answer
3 or not
4 a favor

B 1 answer
2 believe
3 asked
4 arrive

C 1 arrive
2 answer

D 1 ②
2 ②
3 ①
4 ②

Unit 02 bring / call / cause / change

Check the Expressions p.59

bring

1 bring peace
2 brought chaos
3 bring it to an end
4 brought me, joy

call

1 called for
2 call it a day
3 called me names
4 give, a call

Check the Expressions p.61

cause

1 caused, damage
2 causes, disease
3 cause death
4 caused delay

change

1 change my mind
2 changed into
3 change the situation
4 change your attitude

Review the Expressions .... pp.62~63

A 1 peace
2 for
3 delay
4 one's attitude

B 1 brought
2 called
3 cause
4 change

C 1 call
2 change

D 1 ②
2 ①
3 ②
4 ②

Unit 03 close / control / cook / cut

Check the Expressions p.65

close

1 closed my eyes
2 closed my mind to
3 closed an account
4 close to death

control

1 control yourself
2 lost control of
3 under control
4 remote control

Check the Expressions p.67

cook

1 cooked a meal
2 cooked, for dinner
3 cooking breakfast
4 cook it evenly

cut

1 Cut along
2 cutting the lawn
3 cut my finger
4 get my hair cut

Review the Expressions ·········· pp.68~69

A 1 an account
2 oneself
3 a meal
4 the lawn

B 1 closed
2 control
3 cook
4 cut

C 1 control
2 cook

D 1 ②
2 ②
3 ①
4 ②

Unit 04 die / discuss / dream / drop

Check the Expressions ·········· p.71

die

1 died of
2 died for
3 would rather die
4 died a hero

discuss

1 discuss the subject
2 discussed the situation
3 discuss the details
4 discuss how to do

Check the Expressions ·········· p.73

dream

1 dreamed of
2 had a, dream
3 dream, came true
4 vivid dream

drop

1 dropped by
2 dropped the charges
3 dropped a, program
4 dropped off

Review the Expressions ·········· pp.74~75

A 1 a hero
2 the situation
3 comes true
4 a program

B 1 died
2 dropped
3 dream
4 discuss

C 1 discuss
2 dream

D 1 ②
2 ②
3 ①
4 ②

Unit 05 enter / express / face / fall

Check the Expressions ·········· p.77

enter

1 entered the room
2 enter your password
3 enter, college
4 entered into an agreement

express

1 express your opinions
2 express your feelings
3 expressed, interest in
4 express yourself

Check the Expressions ·········· p.79

face

1 facing the, challenge of
2 face the fact
3 face the future
4 faces charges of

fall

1 fell down
2 fell in love with
3 fell asleep
4 fell apart

Review the Expressions ·········· pp.80~81

A 1 into an agreement
2 one's feelings
3 charges of
4 down

B 1 entered
2 express
3 faces
4 fell

C 1 enter
2 face

D 1 ②
2 ②
3 ①
4 ②

Unit 06 feel / gain / help / hold

Check the Expressions ·········· p.85

feel

1 Feel free
2 feel fine
3 felt like
4 how you feel

gain

1 gained independence   2 gain power

3 gained support   4 gain knowledge

Check the Expressions ⋯⋯⋯ p.87

help

1 help out   2 Help yourself to

3 help me with   4 can't help but

hold

1 holding, hands   2 Hold your breath

3 hold tight to   4 hold on to

Review the Expressions ⋯⋯⋯ pp.88~89

A 1 free   2 knowledge

   3 oneself to   4 hands

B 1 felt   2 gained

   3 help   4 Hold

C 1 gain   2 help

D 1 ①   2 ②

   3 ①   4 ①

Unit 07 hope / know / laugh / let

Check the Expressions ⋯⋯⋯ p.91

hope

1 hoping to   2 hope so

3 lose hope   4 full of hope

know

1 know for sure   2 As far as I know

3 is known for   4 If I had known

Check the Expressions ⋯⋯⋯ p.93

laugh

1 laugh at   2 makes me laugh

3 began to laugh   4 tried not to laugh

let

1 Let's see   2 Let me think

3 let's say   4 let go

Review the Expressions ⋯⋯⋯ pp.94~95

A 1 hope   2 for sure

   3 at   4 say

B 1 hoping   2 known

   3 laugh   4 Let

C 1 hope   2 laugh

D 1 ①   2 ②

   3 ②   4 ①

Unit 08 lie / like / look / matter

Check the Expressions ⋯⋯⋯ p.97

lie

1 lie down   2 Lie on your back

3 is lying in   4 tell a lie

like

1 likes to   2 seems like

3 Like I said   4 things like

Check the Expressions ⋯⋯⋯ p.99

look

1 looking at   2 looking for

3 look forward to   4 looks down on

matter

1 matters a lot   2 doesn't matter to

3 All that matters   4 As a matter of fact

Review the Expressions ⋯⋯⋯ pp.100~101

A 1 down   2 someone said

   3 forward to   4 a lot

B 1 lying   2 likes

   3 looking   4 matter

C 1 like   2 matter

D 1 It's nice to lie down on the grass and rest.

  2 It seems like a good idea to me.

  3 The little prince was looking at the sunset.

  4 All that matters is that we're together.

Unit 09 open / pass / pay / play

Check the Expressions ⸻ p.103

open

1 open your heart | 2 opening, accounts
3 Keep your eyes open | 4 open mind

pass

1 pass a test | 2 pass a law
3 pass the time | 4 pass it over

Check the Expressions ⸻ p.105

pay

1 paid for | 2 pay attention to
3 pay in cash | 4 are paid by the hour

play

1 plays an, role | 2 play catch
3 play dead | 4 playing hard to get

Review the Expressions ⸻ pp.106~107

A 1 one's heart | 2 a test
  3 by the hour | 4 dead
B 1 opening | 2 pass
  3 paid | 4 plays
C 1 open | 2 pay
D 1 Keep your eyes open for important details.

  2 If you finish reading a book, you can pass it over to her.

  3 Please pay attention to the road while driving.

  4 I used to play catch with my friends.

Unit 10 put / raise / reach / read

Check the Expressions ⸻ p.109

put

1 put up with | 2 put effort into
3 put me in charge of | 4 put you in danger

raise

1 Raise your hand | 2 raise your voice
3 raised money | 4 raise the alarm

Check the Expressions ⸻ p.111

reach

1 reached a, level | 2 reached a decision
3 reach the age of | 4 reach an agreement

read

1 read aloud | 2 read between the lines
3 read my mind | 4 read it through

Review the Expressions ⸻ pp.112~113

A 1 up with | 2 one's voice
  3 the age of | 4 one's mind
B 1 put | 2 raised
  3 reached | 4 read
C 1 reach | 2 read
D 1 You'll need to put effort into learning English.

  2 Raise your hand if you have a question.

  3 The judge finally reached a decision.

  4 He read between the lines in her messages.

Unit 11 receive / remember / respect / return

Check the Expressions ⸻ p.117

receive

1 received an award | 2 received an invitation
3 receive visitors | 4 received treatment

remember

1 remember well | 2 Remember to
3 hardly remember | 4 As far as I remember

Check the Expressions ····· p.119

respect

1 respect for
2 respect your privacy
3 respect human rights
4 deserves respect

return

1 returned to
2 returned from
3 return my call
4 return the favor

Review the Expressions ····· pp.120~121

A 1 an award
2 someone remember
3 one's privacy
4 the favor

B 1 received
2 Remember
3 respect
4 returned

C 1 remember
2 respect

D 1 I received an invitation from the board.
2 I remember well my first day at school.
3 He deserves respect due to his loyalty.
4 The cleaning robot returned to a charging station.

Unit 12 run / say / set / sit

Check the Expressions ····· p.123

run

1 ran away
2 run for their lives
3 run some tests
4 run in my family

say

1 would say
2 It is said that
3 say so
4 something to say

Check the Expressions ····· p.125

set

1 set a goal
2 set a date
3 set the alarm
4 set the table

sit

1 sit still
2 sit up straight
3 sit down on
4 sits next to

Review the Expressions ····· pp.126~127

A 1 away
2 so
3 a goal
4 down on

B 1 run
2 say
3 set
4 sit

C 1 set
2 sit

D 1 They had to run for their lives to find shelter.
2 It is said that time heals all wounds.
3 People often set a goal on New Year's Day.
4 She asked the children to sit down on the chairs.

Unit 13 start / study / talk / tell

Check the Expressions ····· p.129

start

1 started using
2 start a fight
3 start from scratch
4 start, business

study

1 study hard
2 study for
3 study to be
4 A study shows that

Check the Expressions ····· p.131

talk

1 talk about
2 talk to
3 talk together
4 talked in whispers

tell

1 told us a story
2 told me a secret
3 To tell the truth
4 You never can tell

Review the Expressions ····· pp.132~133

A 1 from scratch
2 hard
3 together
4 the truth

B 1 start
2 studying
3 talk
4 told

C 1 start
2 talk

D 1 We started using online learning platforms.

　2 She helped me study for the midterm.

　3 The children talked in whisper during the game.

　4 My friend told me a secret.

Unit 14 　think / try / turn / wait

Check the Expressions p.135

think

1 thought, hard | 2 think twice
3 Think straight | 4 think big

try

1 try your best | 2 trying something new
3 tried hard | 4 is worth a try

Check the Expressions p.137

turn

1 turned around | 2 turned the corner
3 turn the page | 4 took turns

wait

1 waiting for | 2 wait long
3 waited patiently | 4 can't wait

Review the Expressions .... pp.138~139

A 1 twice | 2 one's best
　3 the corner | 4 long
B 1 think | 2 trying
　3 turned | 4 waited
C 1 think | 2 try
D 1 Think straight before responding to the question.

　2 Learning a new language is worth a try.

　3 We took turns while playing a board game.

　4 Many people were waiting for their turns.

Unit 15 　want / walk / watch / win

Check the Expressions p.141

want

1 wanted me to | 2 might want to
3 wouldn't want to | 4 All I want is

walk

1 walk away | 2 walked out of
3 walk along | 4 walk, dog

Check the Expressions p.143

watch

1 watch TV | 2 Watch out
3 Watch your step | 4 Watch your back

win

1 win a game | 2 win a race
3 winning, war | 4 win, election

Review the Expressions .... pp.144~145

A 1 want to | 2 a dog
　3 out | 4 an election
B 1 wanted | 2 walked
　3 watch | 4 winning
C 1 walk | 2 watch
D 1 All I want is to go on a trip with my friends.

　2 They walked out of the crowds.

　3 Watch your back and stay alert.

　4 They're trying to win a race.

Chapter 3 형용사와 영어표현

Unit 01 bad / big / bright / chilly

Check the Expressions p.151

bad

1 bad habit
2 bad mood
3 bad temper
4 gone bad

big

1 big deal
2 big disappointment
3 big mistake
4 big surprise

Check the Expressions p.153

bright

1 bright color
2 bright future
3 bright idea
4 bright side

chilly

1 chilly morning
2 chilly air
3 chilly wind
4 chilly weather

Review the Expressions .... pp.154~155

A 1 bad habit 나쁜 습관

2 big disappointment 큰 실망

3 bright color 밝은 색
4 chilly air 쌀쌀한 공기

* 답의 순서는 바뀔 수 있습니다.

B 1 in a bad mood
2 a big deal for us

3 the bright side of
4 against the chilly wind

C 1 bad temper
2 big surprise

3 bright idea
4 chilly morning

D 1 bright future / big mistake

누구나 자신을 위한 밝은 미래를 만들어낼 수 있다. 그러나 그 과정에서 실수를 통해 배우는 것이 중요하다. 큰 실수를 저지른다고 해서 세상이 끝나는 것은 아니다.

2 chilly weather / go bad

날씨가 쌀쌀해지면 반드시 따뜻하게 옷을 입어 포근하고

Unit 02 clear / common / deep / direct

Check the Expressions p.157

clear

1 clear message
2 clear understanding
3 make it clear
4 crystal clear

common

1 common language
2 common knowledge
3 common name
4 common enemy

Check the Expressions p.159

deep

1 deep sleep
2 deep trouble
3 deep thought
4 deep breath

direct

1 direct flight
2 direct quote
3 direct experience
4 direct message

Review the Expressions .... pp.160~161

A 1 crystal clear 아주 분명한

2 common enemy 공공의 적

3 deep trouble 심각한 곤경

4 direct message 직접 메시지(DM)

* 답의 순서는 바뀔 수 있습니다.

B 1 make it clear

2 It is common knowledge

3 Take a deep breath

4 through direct experience

C 1 clear understanding
2 common name

3 deep thought
4 direct quote

D 1 deep sleep / direct flight

밖에서 한참 놀고 들어온 어린 여자아이는 깊은 잠에 빠졌고 신비한 모험을 하는 꿈을 꾸었다. 다음 날, 아이의 가족은 테마파크로 향하는 직항 비행기에 태워 아이를 놀라게 했다. 여자아이는 비행기에 탑승해 실제로 모험할 준비를 했다.

2 common language / clear message
각기 다른 배경을 가진 사람들이 함께 모여 상품을 교환하고 이야기를 나누었다. 효과적으로 의사소통하기 위해 그들은 모두가 이해할 수 있는 공용어가 필요했다. 영어는 그들이 생각을 교환하고 명확한 메시지를 전달하는 것을 가능하게 했다.

Unit 03 early / easy / empty / excellnet

Check the Expressions p.163

early

1 early spring	2 early start
3 early days	4 early bird

easy

1 easy money	2 easy questions
3 easy to	4 Take it easy

Check the Expressions p.165

empty

1 empty spaces	2 empty promises
3 feel empty	4 empty-handed

excellent

1 excellent job	2 excellent grades
3 excellent condition	4 excellent choice

Review the Expressions .... pp.166~167

A 1 early bird 일찍 일어나는 사람

2 easy question 쉬운 질문

3 empty promise 공허한[거짓] 약속

4 excellent grade 우수한 성적

* 답의 순서는 바뀔 수 있습니다.

B 1 in early spring

2 easy to understand

3 come back empty-handed

4 in excellent condition

C 1 early start   2 Take it easy

3 feel empty   4 excellent job

D 1 early days / easy money
내가 이 일을 시작한 초창기에는 편하게 돈을 버는 꿈을 꾸곤 했다. 돈 버는 것이 쉽고 단순할 줄 알았던 것이다. 그러나 알면 알수록 돈을 번다는 것은 열심히 일하고 노력해야 가능하다는 것을 깨닫게 되었다.

2 empty space / excellent choice
엠마의 방은 장난감으로 발 디딜 틈이 없었다. 엠마는 정리를 해서 빈 공간을 만들어 내기로 결심했다. 그로 인해 엠마의 방은 더 크고 차분한 느낌이 되었다. 엠마를 행복하게 하고 자신의 결정에 뿌듯함을 느끼게 한 탁월한 선택이었다.

Unit 04 full / front / good / great

Check the Expressions p.169

full

1 full name	2 full moon
3 full-time	4 full of energy

front

1 front page	2 front seat
3 front row	4 in front of

Check the Expressions p.171

good

1 good chance	2 good luck
3 good enough	4 good at

great

1 great success	2 great opportunity
3 great pride	4 great deal of

Review the Expressions .... pp.172~173

A 1 full-time 전업의, 상근의   2 front row 앞줄

3 good enough 만족스러운, 적합한, 충분히 좋은

4 great opportunity 굉장한[멋진] 기회

* 답의 순서는 바뀔 수 있습니다.

B 1 full of energy   2 in front of

    3 gave me a good chance   4 a great deal of

C 1 full name   2 front seat

    3 good at   4 great pride

D 1 full moon / good luck

맑은 날 밤에 보름달이 하늘에서 밝게 빛난다. 많은 이들은 보름달이 행운을 가져다준다고 믿는다. 사람들은 소원을 빌고 좋은 일이 일어나길 바란다.

    2 front page / great success

신문 1면에 그들의 성공이 큰 헤드라인으로 실렸다. 그들은 기쁨과 자부심이 넘쳤다. 모두가 그들의 대성공에 대한 이야기를 흥미롭게 읽었다.

Unit 05 happy / hard / heavy / high

Check the Expressions p.175

happy

1 happy ending   2 happy to

3 happy for you   4 makes me happy

hard

1 had a hard time saying   2 hard to believe

3 hard job   4 hard day

Check the Expressions p.177

heavy

1 Heavy rain   2 heavy traffic

3 heavy workload   4 heavy schedule

high

1 high level   2 high quality

3 high standard   4 high expectations

Review the Expressions .... pp.178~179

A 1 hard job 고된 일

    2 heavy traffic 심한 교통 체증

    3 high standard 높은 수준

    4 happy ending 행복한 결말

    * 답의 순서는 바뀔 수 있습니다.

B 1 was happy to   2 had a hard time

    3 a heavy schedule   4 a high level of skill

C 1 happy for you   2 hard to believe

    3 Heavy rain   4 high quality

D 1 hard day / made me happy

어제는 나에게 힘든 날이었다. 모든 일이 어렵게 느껴졌고 나는 완전히 지쳐버렸다. 그런데 나의 가장 친한 친구가 갑자기 찾아와 날 행복하게 했다. 내 친구의 다정한 말들이 나를 기운나게 했다.

    2 heavy workload / high expectations

나는 새로운 학교에서 공부량이 너무 많다. 끝내야 할 일들도 많다. 우리 선생님들은 내 성적에 대한 기대치가 높다. 나는 최선을 다해 기대에 부응하고 내 역량을 증명해 보일 것이다.

Unit 06 impossible / key / large / long

Check the Expressions p.183

impossible

1 impossible dream   2 impossible mission

3 seems impossible   4 almost impossible

key

1 key issue   2 key role

3 key factor   4 key player

Check the Expressions p.185

large

1 a large amount of   2 a large number of

3 large population   4 large proportion

long

1 long day   2 long way

3 long face   4 as long as

Review the Expressions .... pp.186~187

A 1 long way 먼 곳, 먼 길

    2 large proportion 많은 비율

    3 impossible dream 불가능한 꿈

4 key issue 핵심 논제, 주요 이슈

• 답의 순서는 바뀔 수 있습니다.

B 1 It seems impossible　2 plays a key role in

   3 a large amount of　4 spent a long day

C 1 almost impossible　2 key factor

   3 a large number of　4 as long as

D 1 large population / impossible mission

인구가 많은 어느 대도시에서 용감한 영웅들은 불가능한 임무를 받아들였다. 그들은 도전에 맞서며 사람들에게 희망을 가져다주었다. 그들의 용기는 어떤 것이든 가능하다는 것을 보여 주었다.

   2 key player / long face

보람이는 결승전에서 주전 선수였다. 긴장한 그녀는 실수를 한 것 때문에 울상을 하고 있었다. 그러나 그녀의 선생님은 실수는 일어날 수 있다고 상기시켰다. 선생님의 격려를 받고 그녀는 자신감을 회복했다.

Unit 07　natural / new / personal / quick

Check the Expressions ………………………… p.189

natural

1 natural cause　　2 natural resources

3 natural disasters　4 Natural History

new

1 new generation　　2 new to me

3 new record　　　　4 brand new

Check the Expressions ………………………… p.191

personal

1 personal life　　　　2 personal belongings

3 personal experiences　4 personal use

quick

1 quick decision　　　2 quick response

3 quick sale　　　　　4 quick phone call

Review the Expressions ……………………… pp.192~193

A 1 natural history 자연사, 박물학

   2 personal experience 개인적인[직접] 경험

   3 new record 신기록

   4 quick response 빠른 답변

• 답의 순서는 바뀔 수 있습니다.

B 1 the worst natural disasters

   2 completely new to me

   3 about my personal life

   4 make a quick decision

C 1 natural cause　　　2 brand new

   3 personal belongings　4 quick phone call

D 1 natural resources / new generation

이 세상에는 물, 공기, 나무와 같은 천연자원들이 있다. 천연자원은 생존하는 데 중요하다. 새로운 세대는 더 나은 미래를 위해 이 자원들을 지키고 보존하는 방법을 배워야 한다.

   2 quick sale / personal use

우리가 더 이상 필요하지 않은 물건이 있으면 그것을 판매할 수 있다. 급매란 우리가 그것을 빨리 판매할 수 있음을 뜻한다. 우리는 개인적인 용도를 위해 그 돈을 쓰거나 특별한 무언가를 위해 아껴 둘 수 있다.

Unit 08　rich / serious / severe / steady

Check the Expressions ………………………… p.195

rich

1 rich culture　　　2 rich vocabulary

3 rich soil　　　　4 rich flavor

serious

1 serious illness　　2 serious, problem

3 serious crime　　4 serious threat

Check the Expressions ………………………… p.197

severe

1 severe penalty　　2 severe pressure

3 severe shortage　4 severe weather

steady

1 steady progress   2 steady growth

3 steady person   4 remained steady

Review the Expressions ·········· pp.198~199

A 1 rich vocabulary 풍부한 어휘

   2 serious threat 심각한 위협

   3 steady growth 꾸준한 성장

   4 severe penalty 엄한 처벌

   • 답의 순서는 바뀔 수 있습니다.

B 1 has a rich culture   2 a serious illness

   3 under severe pressure

   4 The weather remained steady

C 1 rich flavor   2 serious crime

   3 severe shortage   4 steady person

D 1 Rich soil / serious problem

   비옥한 토양은 건강한 작물을 재배하는 데 필수적이다. 따라서 토양 오염은 작물에 해를 끼칠 수 있는 심각한 문제이다. 농부들은 유해한 화학 물질의 사용을 자제함으로써 토양을 오염으로부터 보호할 수 있다.

   2 severe pressure / steady progress

   카라는 경주에서 우승해야 한다는 극심한 부담감에 시달리고 있었지만 경기 내내 꾸준히 발전하고 있었다. 그녀는 시작은 느렸지만 점차 속도를 냈다.

Unit 09   strong / terrible / true / valuable

Check the Expressions ·········· p.201

strong

1 strong desire   2 strong influence

3 strong supporter   4 strong opponents

terrible

1 terrible accident   2 in terrible pain

3 terrible mess   4 terrible outcome

Check the Expressions ·········· p.203

true

1 true story   2 true love

3 its true identity   4 true value

valuable

1 valuable lesson   2 valuable information

3 valuable assets   4 valuable time

Review the Expressions ·········· pp.204~205

A 1 strong supporter 확고한 지지자

   2 terrible outcome 최악의 결과(물)

   3 true story 실화

   4 valuable time 값진 시간

   • 답의 순서는 바뀔 수 있습니다.

B 1 had a strong influence

   2 was in terrible pain

   3 true value of friendship

   4 learned a valuable lesson

C 1 strong opponents   2 terrible mess

   3 true identity   4 valuable information

D 1 terrible accident / strong desire

   작은 새 새미는 끔찍한 사고로 날개를 다쳤다. 그러나 새미는 날고자 하는 열망이 있었다. 새미는 절대 포기하지 않았다. 그는 연습하고 믿었다. 그러던 어느 날, 그의 꿈이 이루어져 그는 높이 날아올랐다. 그의 긍정적인 태도는 다른 이들에게도 자극이 되었다.

   2 true love / valuable assets

   사고 이후 나는 진정한 사랑의 힘을 발견했다. 나는 사랑이 기쁨과 행복을 가져다 준다는 것을 알게 되었다. 나는 가족과 친구들이 내 인생에서 가장 소중한 자산임을 깨달았다.

Unit 01 absolutely / deeply / strongly / fully

Check the Expressions ················· p.211

absolutely

1 absolutely wrong   2 absolutely alone

3 absolutely amazed   4 absolutely thrilled

deeply

1 deeply sorry   2 deeply concerned

3 deeply regretted   4 deeply moved

Check the Expressions ················· p.213

strongly

1 strongly disagree   2 strongly suggest

3 strongly recommend   4 strongly criticized

fully

1 fully aware   2 fully awake

3 fully appreciate   4 fully recover

Review the Expressions ··············· pp.214~215

A 1 absolutely wrong   2 deeply regret

 3 strongly criticize   4 fully recover

B 1 absolutely amazed   2 deeply concerned

 3 strongly recommend   4 fully awake

C 1 absolutely thrilled   2 deeply moved

 3 strongly suggest   4 fully appreciate

D absolutely alone / deeply sorry /

strongly disagree / fully aware

A: 그런 무시무시한 집에 나만 혼자 남겨졌다는 게 말이 되나!

B: 맙소사, 진짜 무서웠겠다. 그런 일을 겪어야 했다니 정말 안됐다.

A: 정말 끔찍한 경험이었지만 이젠 끝나서 다행이야.

B: 그런 상황에 누굴 혼자 남겨두는 건 절대 반대야.

A: 지지해 줘서 고마워. 위험성에 대해 충분히 인식은 하고 있었지만 그래도 여전히 어려운 일이었어.

Unit 02 Common adverb collocations

Check the Expressions ················· p.217

1 actively involved   2 badly hurt

3 bitterly cold   4 closely examined

5 completely forgot   6 firmly believe

7 greatly admire   8 happily married

Check the Expressions ················· p.219

1 highly intelligent   2 perfectly normal

3 pretty good   4 quite sure

5 seriously doubt   6 slightly different

7 totally agree   8 widely known

Review the Expressions ··············· pp.220~221

A 1 greatly admire   2 happily married

 3 perfectly normal   4 totally agree

B 1 bitterly cold   2 completely forgot

 3 highly intelligent   4 widely known

C 1 actively involved   2 firmly believe

 3 pretty good   4 slightly different

D badly hurt / closely examine / seriously doubt / quite sure

A: 너 자전거 타다 넘어졌다며. 괜찮아?

B: 나 크게 다쳤어. 의사들이 내 부상 상태를 정밀 진찰해야 된대.

A: 그것 참 안됐네. 학교로 곧 돌아올 수 있겠어?

B: 그건 분명히 어려울 거야. 낫는 데 시간이 걸리긴 할 텐데, 분명히 좋아지긴 할 거야.

A: 빨리 나았으면 좋겠다.